More Praise for *Brilliance by Design*

"This powerful book reminds us that every business, political, or nonprofit le[...] while providing the necessary tools to unleash brilliance in a way that excites, inspires, and empowers our people. *Brilliance by Design* could truly be the difference between success and failure."
—**Betsy Myers, former Executive Director, Harvard Kennedy School Center for Public Leadership**

"This is not a book about just training or teaching. It's about touching lives, creating lasting confidence, and igniting people's innate curiosity. If you are an educator, a consultant, a counselor, or a parent, or if you simply care about the personal and professional development of another, this is a must-read."
—**Christopher Granger, Senior Vice President, Team Marketing and Business Operations, National Basketball Association**

"Teach anyone anything with Vicki's Brilliance Learning System. I LUV it!"
—**Colleen Barrett, President Emeritus, Southwest Airlines, and coauthor of *Lead with LUV***

"No fluff, no fantasy! If you want to expand your influence as a leader, learn from a rock star in the training community how to ENGAGE people. Vicki Halsey delivers a powerful model that works. That's why companies from all over the world are using her approach. If your desire is to increase your ROI on training and create a culture where learning changes lives, *Brilliance by Design* is your blueprint."
—**Kevin and Jackie Freiberg, coauthors of *Nuts!* and *Boom!***

"This book, filled with aha moments, is impossible to put down."
—**Jan Baldwin, Co-CEO, Nth Generation Computing**

"I've had the good fortune to experience Vicki's Brilliance Learning System directly, and I have brought it to WD-40 Company. When given a window into their own brilliance, your people will develop faster, learn more, and innovate at the highest level."
—**Garry Ridge, President and CEO, WD-40 Company, and coauthor of *Helping People Win at Work***

"Vicki leads us to the summit of true enlightenment and expertly shows us how to uncork the brilliance that lies in every person."
—**Simon T. Bailey, author of *Release Your Brilliance***

"Brilliantly written, easily understood, and a model for life-changing impact. Vicki's work with us to offer the San Diego Padres Guest Service Training to a staff of 2,000 employees and follow-up implementation evolved into one of the most talked-about fan experiences anywhere in the world."
—**Richard L. Andersen, CFE, President and CEO, Northlands**

"*Brilliance by Design* presents a proven and powerful educational design strategy. The concepts are simple and the rewards are infinite."
—**Jim Irvine, Manager, Talent Management and Organizational Learning, Nissan North America**

"This book will inspire every educator to engage every learner."
—**Marc Muchnick, author of *No More Regrets!***

"Unmatched in the arena of adult learning, *Brilliance by Design* is the culmination of best practices in one easy, juicy, digestible resource. Like Vicki herself, this book is a gift."
—**Victoria Cabot, Director of Field Operations, Vistage International**

"This book should be required reading for all school administrators and teachers! Vicki blows traditional teaching methods out of the water by exposing a new generation of educational strategies that focus on *delivery* to ensure content mastery."
—**Melissa Holdaway, CEO and President, Arizona Charter Academy**

"If every instructional designer, trainer, and teacher followed Vicki's principles, we'd all be leading richer lives filled with many more brilliant moments of our own."
—**Steve Farber, author of *The Radical Leap and Greater Than Yourself***

"Vicki's 'secret sauce' is in how her ENGAGE process validates the uniqueness of each participant, liberating people to discover their native brilliance and to help others do the same."
—**Larry Ackerman, author of *Identity Is Destiny* and *The Identity Code***

"A must-have for leaders, teachers, and learning departments committed to bringing out the best in people development, learning transfer, and application."
—**Bill Dickinson, Vice President for Sales Training and Development, CareFusion**

"Whether you are a university professor, kindergarten teacher, motivational speaker, or corporate trainer, the multidimensional ENGAGE Model provides powerful insights on how to craft meaningful and life-changing learning experiences."
—**R. Joseph Childs, DBA, Dean, College of Business and Legal Studies, Southeastern University**

"Vicki's passion is clear and contagious—the opening chapters read like a wonderful manifesto for the power of learning."
—**Kevin Eikenberry, author of *Remarkable Leadership***

"To see Vicki facilitate a workshop is to see a master in her element—it's a thing of high energy, optimism, and possibilities. I witnessed the transformative effect her approach had on participants at Save the Children. One of her simple truths, 'The one who is doing the talking is doing the learning,' is a brilliant and real contribution to the learning industry."
—**Justin Birtwell, Director, Global Workforce Learning and Development, Save the Children**

"It's not only being an expert in *what* you teach but also understanding the impact of *how* you teach that can help you change the lives of those you serve. Brilliant, engaging, and powerful."
—Peter Winick, CEO, Thoughtleadershipleverage.com

"Fractal in nature, comprehensive in content, and truly brilliant in design!"
—Shutopa Das, Learning and Performance Coach, Welk Resorts

"Vicki's zest for teaching and bringing out the brilliance in others is absolutely addictive. I know I will have to read this book at least twice and maybe three times to make sure I've dog-eared all the right pages and captured everything I can out of it."
—Brian Hennessy, Learning and Organizational Development Consultant, Sentry Insurance

"As an academic scientist, I know that making discoveries requires that I bring out the brilliance in my students. This book will help me to more effectively teach and lead, whether in one-on-one situations or in large lecture halls."
—Sandra L. Schmid, Professor and Chair, Department of Cell Biology, The Scripps Research Institute

"Amazing, useful, and so needed—this is the book the training world has been waiting for! Vicki's passion for creating supremely effective training comes through in every word."
—Mike Song, CEO, getcontrol.net, and coauthor of *The Hamster Revolution*

"When embraced, the concepts, models, and tools in this book will create a learning environment that will serve employees, drive change, and improve results in any organization."
—Terry McCune, President, K-Tube Corporation

"Vicki's book puts theory into practice and is the most important book you will read as a teacher and learner—period!"
—Bob Lorber, coauthor of *Who Are You? What Do You Want?* and *Putting the One Minute Manager to Work*

"How many boring lectures have we all attended, pretending to watch the speaker but completely tuned out? This never has to happen again. Astutely written, insightful, and utterly practical, *Brilliance by Design* reveals the secrets to optimizing adult learning processes. Vicki writes using the very principles she is explaining. Once I began reading, I couldn't put it down."
—Jesse Stoner, coauthor of *Full Steam Ahead!*

"At Grand Canyon University, students rave about Vicki's sessions. In this book she translates and explains what she does, making it accessible to all who teach."
—Taylor Carr, former Director, Ken Blanchard Executive MBA Program, Grand Canyon University

BRILLIANCE
by
DESIGN

2011

To Chris —

Here's to *your* brilliance

creating learners & leaders

throughout the

world! ☺

Vicki

BRILLIANCE
by
DESIGN

Creating Learning Experiences
That **Connect**, **Inspire**, and **ENGAGE**

VICKI HALSEY

BK

Berrett–Koehler Publishers, Inc.
San Francisco
a BK Business book

Berrett-Koehler Publishers, Inc.
235 Montgomery Street, Suite 650
San Francisco, CA 94104-2916
Tel: (415) 288-0260   Fax: (415) 362-2512   www.bkconnection.com

Ordering Information
Quantity sales. Special discounts are available on quantity purchases by corporations, associations, and others. For details, contact the "Special Sales Department" at the Berrett-Koehler address above.
Individual sales. Berrett-Koehler publications are available through most bookstores. They can also be ordered directly from Berrett-Koehler: Tel: (800) 929-2929; Fax: (802) 864-7626; www.bkconnection.com.
Orders for college textbook/course adoption use. Please contact Berrett-Koehler: Tel: (800) 929-2929; Fax: (802) 864-7626.
Orders by U.S. trade bookstores and wholesalers. Please contact Ingram Publisher Services, Tel: (800) 509-4887; Fax: (800) 838-1149; E-mail: customer.service@ingrampublisher services.com; or visit www.ingrampublisherservices.com/Ordering for details about elec-tronic ordering.

Berrett-Koehler and the BK logo are registered trademarks of Berrett-Koehler Publishers, Inc.

Printed in the United States of America

Berrett-Koehler books are printed on long-lasting acid-free paper. When it is available, we choose paper that has been manufactured by environmentally responsible pro-cesses. These may include using trees grown in sustainable forests, incorporating re-cycled paper, minimizing chlorine in bleaching, or recycling the energy produced at the paper mill.

Library of Congress Cataloging-in-Publication Data

Halsey, Vicki, 1955-
   Brilliance by design : creating learning experiences that connect, inspire, and ENGAGE / Vicki Halsey.
       p. cm.
   Includes bibliographical references and index.
   ISBN 978-1-60509-422-9 (pbk. : alk. paper)
  1. Organizational learning. 2. Learning. 3. Employees—Training of. 4. Effective teaching. I. Title.
   HD58.82.H35 2010
   658.3'124—dc22

                                                                                    2010033502

First Edition

15 14 13 12 11   9 8 7 6 5 4 3 2 1

To Rick, Nick, Jake, Elaine, Charlotte, Nancy,

Ken and Margie,

Johanna, Renee, Margie, Lisa, Kate,

Jenn, Susie, Kathy, Ryan, and Alan,

for seeing me as I am and supporting me always

Contents

Preface

Brilliance by Design will show you how to bring passion, relationship, purpose, and success to every learning opportunity. It captures the best of what I've learned from mentors, friends, students, and colleagues through my 35 years of helping people learn and creating high-impact instructional design. It combines that knowledge with 20+ years of brain and learning behavioral research to arm you with hundreds of new strategies and practices to add to your repertoire. *Brilliance by Design* will help you align your best intentions with your methods and objectives and mobilize passionate learners to get amazing results.

Extreme Engagement

The secret to powerful instruction is engagement—involving learners in activities in which they do the work of interacting with new content, wrestling with concepts, and teaching those concepts to others. Learner-centered classrooms, training rooms, and meeting rooms—wherever learning is happening—are noisy and alive with energetic activity as learners think out loud, build knowledge, conceive their own models for understanding, and practice applying those models. The learners talk more while the teacher talks and presents less. As people hear their own voices and engage in challenges designed to help them understand at deeper levels, they learn by teaching. They access more of their potential and contribute at higher levels, resulting in retention and application over time. In this dynamic world, the teacher's job is to engage learners in myriad ways: to connect them to ideas and skills, challenge them and support their accruing knowledge, celebrate their brilliance, and help them apply their learning to real-world situations. In teaching, you consciously connect in order to engage, and you engage in order to create new meaning, beliefs, and behaviors.

> It is rigorous work that energizes both learners and teachers and builds continuously on deep connections.

Brilliance Is a Trajectory

When my son Nicholas came home from his first year at college, he was clearly excited about everything he had experienced—but all he could talk about was how he had nailed a particular question on one of his finals. I heard him share with his dad how he masterfully pulled a discrete fact from his brain and figured out the trick in the question. He also shared his insight with me, the neighbors, two friends, and with his grandmother on the phone. If you were to call him, I am sure he would share it with you, too.

Every parent wants his or her child to feel brilliant. As I listened to Nick, however, I was struck by how rare it is to hear that kind of joy in one's outpouring of creativity and genius. We hear people talk about sports, movies, the weather, or what they had for dinner, but seldom about the times when they felt brilliant. What series of events leads to learning moments where everything clicks and comes together—the right information, powers of observation, and the ability to think and articulate those thoughts?

I realized that *brilliance is a trajectory.* It is a relationship filled with requests, clear expectations, mindful practice, and learning over time. Nick's ability to answer the test question came from a carefully orchestrated combination of clear information, hard work, and learning from lectures, DVDs, practical labs, and peer study groups. The integration of each of these activities allowed him to confidently weave a quarter's worth of acquired knowledge from a variety of sources into brilliance. *It was brilliance, designed.*

Replace "Sit 'n' Get" with "Woo 'n' Do"

What distinguishes *Brilliance by Design* from most books on learning is that it contains a specific instructional design model that revolutionizes typical teaching methods. It upturns the passive "sit 'n' get" format ingrained in our culture and replaces it with a proven model for optimal learning that "woos" people as they "do" the work. I share in these pages my secrets, tips, tools, and strategies as well as stories of my successes and failures and what I learned from them. I invite you to take this information and use it to unleash the brilliance in others, achieve powerful outcomes, and build communities of learners—confident learners who will share best practices and communicate at a deep and profound level as they take your content out into the world and do the real work to transform it.

Brilliance by Design articulates a three-part system—the Brilliance Learning System:

- Part 1 focuses on strategies to develop your *content,* or **what** you are going to teach;

- Part 2 helps you gain a deeper understanding of the **people** in the learning equation (learners and teachers), or **who** you want to learn; and

- Part 3 gives you hundreds of ideas to implement each aspect of the six-step ENGAGE Learning Design Model that, when followed, is **how** you are going to unleash brilliance.

To help inspire and facilitate your ability to move key concepts to action, please interact with the content of the book and complete the activities, questions, and challenges. This will help you gain a deeper awareness of your thoughts, generate greater meaning, and move the learning to high-impact application.

Brilliance Is Not a Random Act

Brilliance is not a random act. It is the result of learning over time—having the space to dig deep into preexisting learning and combine it with new knowledge, resulting in unique thoughts. It is about people, content, and a structure for learning designed to connect, inspire, and engage.

Learning is a deep, compelling human connection. It is the gateway to optimal life experiences. Learning *transforms people's lives.* And teaching, in any forum, is the art and science of bringing out the brilliance that drives those transformations.

> Teaching, in any forum, is the art and science of bringing out the brilliance that drives transformations.

People are naturally brilliant in their own unique ways. Our brilliance—our intelligence, talent, skills, and creativity—resides close to the surface, waiting to emerge through inspiration and rigorous work. This process of connecting with our innate brilliance to further our learning also connects us to the best in ourselves and the best in others. It empowers us and makes us feel alive. It is the extraordinary privilege of a teacher—and by *teacher* I want to be clear that this means *anyone* who seeks to bring out the best in others—to facilitate the full potential, the brilliance, of every learner in every learning situation.

The Tragedy of Too Few Brilliant Moments

The last time I trained at a Fortune 100 company, during our break I walked past the doorway of a nearby training room and glanced in at the participants. They reminded me of characters in the old movie *Invasion of the Body Snatchers*: glazed faces, blank stares—people sitting motionless and looking at a PowerPoint slide show while a well-meaning instructor talked a blue streak.

In the workplace today and in classrooms around the world, there are too many opportunities to leave our brains at the door and too few opportunities for brilliance. People are asked to come to meetings or training with no advance notice about what is going to be discussed and no opportunity to prepare. Then they are expected to provide meaningful input into key decisions and outcomes that will impact the organization long into the future. We give them huge notebooks of information and, after quickly reviewing it with them, expect them to remember it all and instantly put the concepts into action. And we are consistently disappointed when they do not immediately close new business or use the information accurately. In short, we often set people up to fail, and then we are irritated when they do.

Unlock Brilliance in Any Situation

So how can you create more opportunities for people to unleash their brilliance? *Brilliance by Design* shows you a proven, powerful educational design for creating optimal learning experiences every time you teach by using a learner-centered and active—not passive—approach. It revolutionizes typical teaching methodologies to get your learners sitting on the edge of their seats and eagerly anticipating learning.

In the early years of my career as a teacher, counselor, and school administrator, I worked with kids from every walk of life—from children of famous scientists to the toughest, most challenging gang members. From juvenile detention centers to jails, from gifted and special education classrooms to after-school detention and study groups, I helped kids find success when others had given up. In my current role as Vice President of Applied Learning at The Ken Blanchard Companies, I write, teach, and deliver powerful learning systems for corporate clients like Nike, Wells Fargo-Wachovia, Gap, Microsoft, and GlaxoSmithKline while teaching executive leadership courses at two universities. Like you, my role changes day to day, minute to minute. No matter what role you or I play in life, when it comes right down to it, to be highly successful, each of us needs to be a learner *and* a teacher. The circular energy that arises from the mutuality of teaching and learning is a powerful, fulfilling connection.

Each Person Has a Unique Contribution

From the classroom to the boardroom, learning starts with the fundamental fact that each person exists to make a unique contribution to the world.

Every teacher needs to find a way to reach joyfully into the soul of learners and facilitate their brilliance so that they can make their contributions. It is my hope that *Brilliance by Design* will help you pursue and achieve that transformational goal.

The Brilliance Learning System Applies to Any Learning Situation

The Brilliance Learning System is fractal in nature. You can use it to teach in any learning situation, including but not limited to classrooms, meetings, workshops, and keynote speeches. You can use it to coach one person at a time, to facilitate a virtual sales meeting with your global team, to train a roomful of people at all levels in an organization, or to give a keynote address to thousands. The core principles apply equally well regardless of the amount of time: forty-minute meetings, hour-long keynotes, or four-day training sessions. This system helps anyone who brings people together for the purpose of learning, problem solving, or innovating to develop a clear, high-impact training design; analyze learner and teacher needs; create objectives that meet those needs; incorporate interactive tools that "fire 'em up"; ensure compliance with all key outcomes; and send people out into the world feeling empowered to change their lives.

Preview of What's Ahead: The Book at a Glance

The introduction, "The Time for Brilliance Has Come" relates stories of inspirational teachers who have had a profound impact, takes a close look at how and why these teachers were so remarkable, and describes the three parts of the Brilliance Learning System: People, Content, and Learning Design.

Chapter 1, "Fire Up the Synergy between Learners and Teachers," explains the power of a highly collaborative relationship and explores in detail the first component of the Brilliance Learning System: People. You will learn about the revolutionary premise *Whoever is doing the teaching is doing the learning* as well as the three pivotal 70/30 Principles that rebalance the learning equation and reframe the mindset of the teacher. You also will learn how to leverage compelling human connections to inspire intellectual passion while catalyzing your own strengths and the strengths of your learners.

In **Chapter 2**, you will learn to "Craft Content That Sings" and commit to the second component of the Brilliance Learning System: Content. The clarity of your content, crafted into a meaningful model, can be a power tool for interactive, retainable learning. Presenting it in digestible pieces and through concrete examples sets learners up for success and makes recall attainable. You'll read true stories that illustrate how important it is to tap into and sometimes shift learners' beliefs in order for them to be open to new learning.

The third component of the Brilliance Learning System, Learning Design, is detailed in **Chapters 3 through 9**. Chapter 3 is a quick overview of the ENGAGE Model. It will help you see the total flow and structure to enable you to bring out the brilliance in others. The subsequent chapters walk you through the model step by step for a deeper look and a chance to move your learning to action through templates and activities.

Chapters 4 through 9 also expand on each of the six steps of the ENGAGE Model. These chapters give you hundreds of ideas, strategies, and practices for how to energize and value learners, make knowledge accessible and meaningful, assess and celebrate learning, and apply and extend the learning in their lives. I will share with you a treasure trove of learning activities for all types of learners, the basis for multiple approaches, and tips and insights, tested over time, that I have developed myself or learned and borrowed from my many brilliant teachers.

Chapter 10, "Bringing Out Brilliance in the Virtual Classroom," shows you how to take advantage of digital technology so that you will be able to more specifically connect, inspire, and engage the online learner. It overflows with creative tools and strategies for maximizing learning in the virtual classroom and it focuses on the power of connecting learners to their core purpose.

> Tap all opportunities.

A Great Teacher Is Like a Great Athlete

While it may not be intuitive to be a great teacher, it is something you can learn. If you use the Brilliance Learning System and the ENGAGE Model, you will develop your abilities and ensure your successes. You will learn to impart information in a way that consistently improves your skill and helps you align your intentions with your efforts. You will send your learners out the door armed with tools and strategies for applying their new knowledge in their lives when they need it. Being a great teacher is like being a great athlete: It is a constant challenge, but if you are willing to learn and grow, you can keep getting better. Hard work and practice make all the difference in the kind of learning that transforms lives.

The Time for Brilliance Has Come

S tand and Deliver is the story of Jaime Escalante, a mathematics teacher in an East Los Angeles high school who challenged his students to achieve greatness. He dared to teach with the intention of ensuring that not only would all his students graduate from high school, but also any who aspired to go to college could go. He dedicated himself to teaching his pupils how to strive and inspiring them to learn in order to reach their fullest potential.

Escalante employed innovative teaching methods that attracted the students' attention, sparked their intelligence, and, most importantly, transformed their lives by changing their beliefs about their own talents and capabilities. Despite a wall of disapproval and disbelief, Escalante worked tirelessly to create a safe, respectful environment that constantly challenged the students to work harder, dig deeper, and reach higher plateaus of learning. Ultimately, they proved their worth to themselves and to others by passing their Advanced Placement Calculus exams in record numbers, which helped them break through the ceiling of limitations in their lives. How did Escalante do it? How did one teacher defy all odds, facilitate learning potential, and help his students transform their lives?

Be a Vision of Hope

Escalante created a mindset and a vision of hope that clearly valued learning in his classroom by consciously structuring his lessons and believing in the *brilliance* of his students. His deliberate learning design and genuine belief in their capabilities reframed their thinking, ignited their self-esteem, connected them to meaningful learning, and engaged them in rigorous practice to make newly acquired knowledge their own. Escalante envisioned them as hardworking students, aspiring learners, and high achievers. Then he held up the mirror so his students could see in themselves what he saw in them.

Brilliance Is a Relationship

As I read about Jaime Escalante's students claiming their brilliance and the rewards of their hard-earned success, I felt a welling of emotions—triumph, pride, inspiration, and renewed hope—that came from a core conviction we all know: *Brilliance happens when someone—a teacher, mentor, speaker, leader, coach, colleague, manager, or teammate—facilitates the talents and capabilities inside us that are waiting to emerge, helps us rise to seemingly impossible heights, and challenges us at a deep level so that we, as Learners (with a capital L), demonstrate that we can reach the summit, conquer all barriers, and unleash our brilliance over and over again.* Escalante was that teacher, that leader, for his students and his community.

Who was yours? Who was your Jaime Escalante, your teacher or inspiration—the person whose influence awakened you to reframe your thinking about yourself and your life, to see yourself and to reimagine your future with new eyes?

For me, it was David Wilson, American Studies professor at the University of California–Davis. Despite my well-practiced modus operandi—doing assigned readings, discerning what the professor wanted me to learn and regurgitating it, hanging in the background and not standing out in any way, and giving most learning endeavors only a fraction of my energy—David Wilson got to me. One day, I stayed after class with a few other students to ask about an upcoming project. True to form, I let the others take charge and do the talking while I hid behind them, assuming they were smarter and more capable of speaking up and taking the lead. Truth be told, I barely listened, knowing that one of my friends would fill me in. As we were leaving, suddenly, I heard my name. "Vicki, I'd like to talk with you for a few minutes if you have time." Red-faced and feeling the uncomfortable instantaneous presence of a cold sweat, I realized that I was no longer under the radar.

Wishing I could shrink like Alice in Wonderland and slip through a rabbit hole, I mustered courage and said, "Yes, sir."

Are You Bringing Out Brilliance?

Professor Wilson asked me a question I'll never forget—a question that changed my world and helped me to see myself through his eyes: "How are we going to bring out the brilliance in you?" I was stumped. Brilliant? Me? But there he was, looking at me as if I were brilliant and expecting an answer. I tried what always had worked for me in the past—staying safe and muttering what I figured he wanted me to say. Suddenly, he slammed his hand on his desk and said, "I'm not interested in hearing what you think I want to hear; I want to know what *you* think. *You.*" Long, strained moments passed while he sat there staring at me, waiting for a reply. It was painful. I started to cry, knowing he had touched something inside me that I had suppressed for a long time. He gave me a tissue and really looked at me, still waiting, still expecting an answer. Finally, this wise, masterful teacher shared his vision of two different Vickis: one in class who withheld genius, and one outside of class who revealed her genius through the powerful insights she wrote in her papers. It was time, he said—time to bring out my brilliance.

And now it's time for you to bring out the brilliance in the thousands of others who are hiding, hoping to stay under the radar, not realizing how much they have been limiting their potential by diffusing their vision. Ask yourself: What percentage of people's brilliance am I unleashing in meetings, seminars, workshops, and keynotes? Think about it. What percentage of their full capability are people generating in your learning experiences? Are people sitting up, speaking out, asking great questions, and applying their learning as fast as they can? Or are they lying low, physically present and seemingly alert but content to listen as you do all the hard work?

> Ask yourself: What percentage of people's brilliance am I unleashing in meetings, seminars, workshops, and keynotes?

Exercise: Inspiring Brilliance

It's time to pick up your pen and unleash inspiration. Let's get started right now.

Writing is a great way to get your energy flowing, to explore, and to see things in a new way. Take notes right in this book or in a separate notebook. Scribble away! Feel free to use your computer and let your fingers fly as you ponder and respond to the following revealing questions. Jot down some notes for each one, or read them a few times and write a short personal story. The writing doesn't have to be perfect; just meaningful for you. If writing feels like a barrier, talk out loud. Record your ideas with any recording device. What's important is that you *do the hard work* of being totally present with your thoughts and emotions by recording or writing them down. This is the first step in connecting the intellectual rigor with the emotional engagement that unlocks brilliance in yourself and others.

REFLECTION: Exercise

INSPIRING BRILLIANCE

- Who has seen the brilliant you? Who helped you see yourself in a different light?

- Who gave you the opening you needed to become who you are?

- Who lives in your mind as a great teacher?

- What did this person do to inspire you?

- What did this person do to help you see yourself in a new way, accept a challenge, and be all you could be?

- What stand out in your mind as key strategies that triggered your drive?

- How has this influence or learning shown up and endured in your life?

- Why is this important to you today—right now?

Awaken the Purpose

Professor Wilson's poignant question woke me up. I was going through the motions, disconnected from myself and what was important to me. He was the spark that fired me up to do the focused work of figuring out who I am, what matters to me, and how I wanted those things to show up in my life. The resulting self-awareness connected me to my passion for learning and teaching. Without him, I might have spent my whole life playing it safe.

Each individual is a unique combination of talents and life experiences. It's easy for gifts or talents to become temporarily or even permanently lost in the litany of perceived expectations and obligations on any given day. David Wilson forced me to connect more authentically to myself; every day since, I've realized a little more of my talent and skill in teaching and that designing high-impact learning initiatives is my passion. We all thrive on watching others come alive through learning and moving their learning into action. The skill of teaching is not innate in everyone, but bringing out the best in others *can* be learned. As teachers, our core purpose is to unleash brilliance—to facilitate greatness in others directly in every learning situation we lead and indirectly by training others in the art and science of teaching.

Together we can help people claim their greatness, and we can create stimulating, safe environments that facilitate the gifts of a multitude of learners so that each of them can discover and feel what it is like to make a unique contribution while moving through his or her daily life.

> Help people claim their greatness.

Design a Structure That Supports Optimal Learning

Now is the time to leverage optimal learning practices. People who have a hint of curiosity await the opportunity to challenge themselves to greater meaning in their lives through new learning. Tired of sitting mindlessly in virtual or physical classrooms, meetings, or trainings, many learners are rebelling. They are finding their own ways to stimulate their brains through multitasking or going on vacations of the mind; in other words, they are showing up physically but checking out mentally. Successful people in all aspects of life and in all levels of organizations seek new learning to be current and competitive and to thrive as high performers.

A 2006 article in *Training Journal* reported results from a study in the United Kingdom that showed 80 percent of workers "believe training is the key to developing their careers despite many being unhappy with the quality of sessions provided." The same study of 500 businesses and 1,300 staff also found "more than three-quarters of workers see training as a key benefit when looking for a job." This research, which was part of a broader study in Europe of more than 1,000 businesses and 4,000 workers from Britain, France, and Germany, found similar results in all three countries.[1]

Your challenge: Capture the attention of these learners. Make a sacred pact. Teach and help them learn new content in a way that fully engages them and makes it possible for them to use this knowledge, do their best work, and build lasting results. At the same time, you will be creating empowered communities and organizations of strong individuals armed with new, life-changing knowledge. Like Jaime Escalante, are you determined and ready to seize the moment, to rebalance the learning equation in order to unlock brilliance in your learners and teach them so that they learn at a higher level? Your learners are. They are waiting for you.

Brilliance Learning System: How It Works

The Brilliance Learning System, represented in Figure I.1, is an educational system that will help you structure your teaching so that you maximize every learning opportunity for yourself and your learners. The system is based on three essential components that work together:

- The WHO: People (Learners and Teachers)
- The WHAT: Content (Ideas and Information)
- The HOW: ENGAGE Learning Design Model (Strategies and Tools)

Each of these components is distinct and important. However, their true strength and effectiveness are in their relationship with each other. As learners and teachers, we can do a lot to be our best and bring out the best in others. We can prepare our content so that it is accessible, interesting, and meaningful. And we can ENGAGE learners and immerse them in the content by means of a learning design that includes strategies and tools that support their absorption of knowledge and extend to successful application.

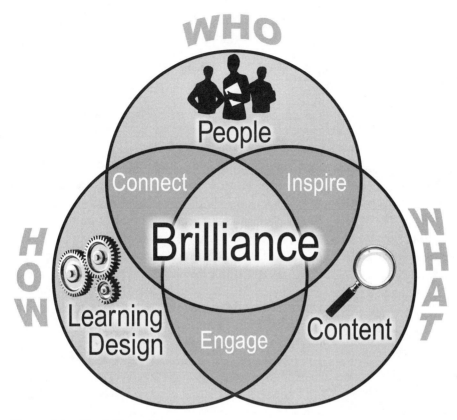

Figure I.1. The Brilliance Learning System

Energy Drives Learning

Let's look at Figure I.1 again. Notice the words in the intersecting triangles that form where the circles overlap: Connect, Inspire, and Engage. These core elements emerge with the intersection of the WHO, the WHAT, and the HOW. They set in motion and sustain the all-important flow of energy that produces vital relationships, fires up the brilliance zone in learners, and results in optimal learning experiences. You and your learners *connect* with each other and the content in many ways and on many levels. You continuously *inspire* and then *engage* your learners. This cycle is an unending process throughout the ENGAGE Model, and it is vital to the Brilliance Learning System.

Just as our blood circulates through our bodies in an intentional, continuous flow that sustains our life, the Brilliance Learning System sets in motion a learning energy that cycles in a constant stream and builds enthusiasm, openness, active involvement, meaning, and knowledge. It maximizes our openness to learning. This openness and engagement moves us to greater depths of understanding so that ultimately learners embody the knowledge and make it their own. The powerful language and practice will free innate knowledge to connect to the new learning and release more clarity about how to move forward with this new understanding.

The ENGAGE Model

At the heart of the effectiveness of the Brilliance Learning System is the ENGAGE Model, the Learning Design component. The most salient principle of the model is what I think of as a radical shift or revolution in how we think of most classroom models: Whoever is teaching is doing the learning. Therefore, the ENGAGE Model is rich with abundant opportunities for learners to practice through teaching, actively building their own knowledge. Your role is to facilitate learning. You start as the "master teacher," but your main role is to give enough information to enable the learner to work with and practice the new content. As you take a step back into the role of coach or guide, the learners themselves begin to teach the new content, garnering a deeper understanding, building confidence, releasing their brilliance, and making the new knowledge their own. Through this highly interactive process, you catalyze your learners to master the content you present so they can take their newly attained knowledge out into the world, generate enthusiasm for it, apply it, practice it, and avidly teach and share it—thereby maximizing your content and extending your reach.

> Whoever is teaching is doing the learning.

Learning Fuels Life

Learning is a constant in our lives—a continuous journey. It requires self-discipline, dedication, hard work, and practice. Be forewarned. As with any evolution that involves change, this endeavor will not be easy. It is hard work. Like Jaime Escalante, it will require you to be relentless and mindful, positive and joyful. People will come to you eager and impatient for more—because once they experience being their best and bringing out brilliance in others, they will not settle for less.

CHAPTER **1**

Fire Up the Synergy between Learners and Teachers

Dale Chihuly is a renowned glass sculptor. His bold, colorful pieces come from a range of influences and include simple and exotic forms found in nature such as spheres and cylinders, sea creatures, and desert cacti. You can see them in museums, office buildings, hotels, and outdoor landscapes around the world. However, his most exciting contribution to the art glass world has to be his extraordinarily innovative idea of bringing together teams of artists with exceptional glassblowing abilities to create large-scale, spectacular glass sculptures. Led by Chihuly's vision and direction, these casts of collaborators engage in highly physical, dramatic productions in which they create pieces that result from the synergy of all the artists' specialized skills. By combining their talents, these teams collectively produce unique art pieces that would not otherwise come into being.[1]

This artistic collaboration is a powerful analogy to the synergy that evolves during the teaching and learning process that unleashes brilliance. Each of us brings our individual talents, skills, and knowledge to the process. Just as Chihuly does, the teacher leads with purpose and vision. But the outcome—the unique learning and results for each individual you influence—is completely dependent upon each learner's willingness to join in as collaborator in the experience. Establishing this valuable teacher-learner relationship is an art and an essential ingredient to everyone's success.

Synergy Gets Results

Synergy is all about working together and supporting each other's success. A quick look in the dictionary tells us that synergy means "joint work, to work together, combined or cooperative action or force."[2] Wikipedia says "A synergy is where different entities cooperate advantageously for a final outcome. If used in a business application it means that teamwork will produce an overall better result than if each person was working toward the same goal individually . . . a dynamic state in which combined action is favored over the difference of individual components."[3] Take a moment to think again of Dale Chihuly's team of glassblowers. They are fired up, working together toward a common objective, bringing their individual strengths and talents forward, and supporting each other's work—everyone contributing to create the resulting masterpiece. Your outcome will not take the form of a glass sculpture that looks like a sea anemone or octopus. It will, however, take form as crystallized knowledge and empowered skills in the minds and practices of your learners, and it will fuel productivity as well as individual, community, and organizational vitality. All this arises from the unique synergistic relationship you create with your learners throughout your learning session.

The Brilliance Learning System Starts with People: Learners and Teachers

The first component, and the foundation of the Brilliance Learning System, is people who create synergistic relationships. These relationships between learners and teachers can be defining and life changing. They can and must bring out the best in us and the best in others. Jaime Escalante in Los Angeles and my teacher David Wilson at UC Davis established relationships with their students that made them shift their beliefs, join in a common objective, and work extremely hard to meet high standards. Thomas Friedman, journalist, Pulitzer Prize winner, and author of best-selling books including *The World Is Flat*, once paid homage in a *New York Times* column to his high school journalism teacher, Hattie Steinberg. Friedman, who credited Steinberg with "inspiring in him a love of reporting and news-papers," took her Introduction to Journalism course in 1969 and never took, or felt he needed to take, another journalism class. In his column he de-scribed Hattie Steinberg as tough and "a woman of clarity in an age of un-certainty." He explained that he and other students hung out in Steinberg's room "as if it were a malt shop," not because it was cool but because they "enjoyed being harangued by her, disciplined by her, and taught by her." Friedman voiced his respect for his teacher and his gratitude for the lasting impact her lessons had on his life. He wrote, "I sit up straight just thinkin' about her."[4] It sounds like Hattie Steinberg was as formidable and demand-ing as Jaime Escalante and as inspiring and courageous as David Wilson. She no doubt reminds you, at least a little, of a great teacher from whom you learned enduring truths.

When it comes down to it, inspired teachers who get their students to work hard and join them in a collaborative process are people we want to be around. We trust them. They demand a lot from us, but they also give a lot of themselves. Their enthusiasm for life ignites our own. They make learning safe by turning mistakes into opportunities for learning. They cre-ate an environment of trust and mutual respect. They design and imple-ment strategies for rigorous work and risk taking that we value. We work harder because we want to.

Learners trust teachers who demonstrate their authenticity and reliabil-ity. Their words and actions are in alignment; they walk the talk. So when a teacher says, "This learning experience is about you, and you are going to learn X, Y, and Z," that teacher is creating a learner-centered experience and indicating, quickly and persistently, that X, Y, and Z will be learned. Great synergies come from mutuality. The teacher creates an environment in which everyone really "shows up" and brings their best to the endeavor.

So how do you ensure that everyone brings their best to the endeavor? How do you align your best intentions with the learning design?

Rebalance the Learning Equation: The 70/30 Principle

Rebalancing the learning equation is a great way to start. In *Leadership from the Inside Out*, Kevin Cashman describes two different approaches he calls "streams of leadership." One is an "extremely hard-driving . . . 'I' leader who gets results." The other is a "more interpersonally connected . . . collab-orative and synergistic . . . 'We' leader." Cashman explains that individuals, teams, and organizations thrive when we develop both the *I* and the *We* qualities in our leadership style.[5]

These two streams of leadership are as applicable and important in any learning situation as they are in leadership. To practice and enable the kind of learning that unlocks brilliance, we need to be vigilant about the dynamics of the *I* and the *We*. There is greater synergy when the space is created for everyone to step forward to perform in a tidelike rhythm and motion of exchange—a rolling back and forth where the teacher steps forward more forcefully, then steps back and makes space for the powerful voices and contributions of the learners. This demands a shift in teaching style and a letting go somewhat of ego. We've all heard the expression "Leave your ego at the door." This is a reminder that the possibilities inherent in highly synergistic relationships are only achievable in an environment where everyone's voice and contribution is heard and where everyone has the opportunity to develop. By letting go of ego, we also let go of judging people,

Learners become teachers.

including ourselves. This is important because when we feel better than or less than someone else, we are separating ourselves from others and may miss opportunities to connect with them.

Close your eyes for a moment. Place yourself in a traditional learning situation. What's happening? The teacher is at the front of the room, right? Who is doing the talking? The teacher, right? Who is standing, moving around the room? Who is engaged with the ideas and the information? Whose voice do you hear most of the time? Who's excited? The teacher, the teacher, and the teacher. I created the Brilliance Learning System to revolutionize that learning model. It is based on this key premise: *Whoever is doing the talking is doing the learning.*

A shift in focus will help you rebalance the learning equation, place the spotlight on the learners, engender active rather than passive learning, and change how you teach so that you and the learners really do bring the best to the endeavor and bring out brilliance. Three shifts support the 70/30 Principle.

Shift 1:
Learners Do 70 Percent of the Talking and 30 Percent of the Listening

The goal of the 70/30 Principle is for your learners to feel that they are at the center of the learning session and to get them actively learning. You can make this happen by shifting your focus from doing most of the talking and teaching (which often amounts to about 70 percent) to doing far less (about 30 percent). This establishes a more learner-centered focus and ensures greater ownership and success for the learner. It spotlights the *learner*, not you, as the focus of the learning session.

> Be the guide on the side versus the sage on the stage.

Shift 2:
Teachers Dedicate 70 Percent of Their Preparation to How (Learning Design) and 30 Percent to What (Content) They Will Teach

It is common in most teacher-learner situations for the teacher to focus 70 percent of his or her time on preparing content and 30 percent on figuring out how to teach that content. With the Brilliance Learning System, we reverse that focus now and forevermore! *Commit yourself to focusing 30 percent of your time and energy on deciding* what *your objectives are, what key takeaways*

From:	To:
70% **you** talk/teach	70% **they** talk/do
70% **what** you are going to teach	70% **how** you are going to teach it
70% of time you **teach** skills	70% of time learners **practice/build** skills

Figure 1.1. Rebalancing the Learning Equation—the 70/30 Principle

you want for your learners, and what *visuals you want to use, and 70 percent of your time and energy on* how *you will create activities and embed best learning practices.*

That 70 percent effort goes into applying the ENGAGE Model, which I will walk you through in subsequent chapters. Learning Design, or *how* you teach, is the stage on which the learning story takes place, and it is the carefully planned central plot. It needs to be packed full of interactive learning opportunities and activities.

Shift 3:
Learners Spend 30 Percent of the Time Learning and 70 Percent of the Time Practicing

Since learners are the stars of the play—the main characters on the learning event stage—they get to have most of the lines and action, which means they get to have a lot of time to practice new skills and information. In traditional learning models, teachers typically spend 70 percent of the learning event time teaching skills, and learners spend only 30 percent practicing those skills. As you see yourself more as the director of talented people who want to shine and produce amazing results, you realize that the more they practice, the greater their chance for success when they are on their own. *Learners need to spend 70 percent of the total learning event time practicing the new skills, working with them, and teaching others, while you spend only 30 percent of the time teaching the skills to them* (Figure 1.1).

Create a Continuous Flow of Connections

How can we ensure that everyone brings his or her best to the endeavor? How can we bring out the brilliance in ourselves and in learners as we work toward objectives?

In addition to the 70/30 Principle, another way to rebalance the learning equation is to establish a learner-centered mindset. This is an important underpinning of a more synergistic style of learning. When you walk through the chapters regarding the use of the ENGAGE Model, you will see how this is put into practice through many conscious choices. You also will see that each of these choices is necessary to create a continuous flow of connections. You want to connect learners to themselves by inspiring and celebrating who they are—their capabilities and contributions. You want to connect them to their purpose and hopes, and their sense of community. You also want to connect them to your content and to its meaning and application. As you work to make these connections, *your* energy fuels *their* energy to embody and embrace your content because of its deeper connection to who they are and what they want to become. You have reinforced and put into language what they know to be true. The cycle is constant, demanding, and energizing. Everyone feels a sense of fulfillment. Powerful relationships form between the teacher and learners and also within the group of learners itself. This is a powerful paradigm for learning, and much of it arises by nurturing a mindset that starts with you—who you are as the teacher and the contribution you bring to your learners—and radiates to how you feel about your learners: your genuine belief that you want them to succeed.

Brilliance Starts with You

Brilliance starts with you, the teacher—your mindset and your investment. Both of these factors are crucial in catalyzing your strengths and those of your learners. Developing your learner-centered mindset, belief in learner success, and commitment to creating learning experiences that support that success are critical, so it is important to invest in yourself as well as your learners. You might think of preparing for learning events as you would prepare for an athletic event such as a marathon, triathlon, or even an Olympic event. Being your healthiest, strongest, most skilled and talented self requires many layers of training and practice. Such a demanding and exciting process begins, like anything else, with a willingness to do the work of learning more about yourself and connecting with or working synergistically with others. In the rest of this chapter we'll explore how you can consciously develop a mindset that supports optimal learning and how you can consciously invest in yourself and your learners to bring out brilliance.

Know Yourself

While it is important that you be the expert in your content, it is perhaps more important that you know, constantly learn about, and accept yourself. Self-awareness is the cornerstone of emotional intelligence and is essential for authentically growing into your full potential as an individual, a teacher, and a leader. It also is the foundation for connecting authentically with your learners.

REFLECTION: Exercise

KNOWING YOURSELF

In an ideal world, some of the first work you do as a teacher is reflection and self-awareness. If you have done something like this before, that's great—but there is always more to discover. Take the time to think about the following important questions. Write down your answers in a notebook or record them as an audio file. Date your entries and save them. Try to do this exercise at least once a year.

- Who am I?
- What is important to me?
- What are my gifts and strengths?
- What are some areas that need improvement?
- What inspires and motivates me?
- What are my goals? (What do I want to achieve?)
- What are barriers to my goals?
- What are my passions?
- What is my purpose?
- What energizes me?
- What do I need to sustain my passion, my purpose, and my energy?
- What have I done recently that makes me happy?
- How could I do more of that?
- What has become clearer to me after answering these questions?
- How do I best learn?

Connect with Self and Others

The drive for self-awareness is motivated not only by a personal desire for continued learning and growth (which fuels happiness), but also by the knowledge that the more self-aware people are, the more fully they can connect with others and their experiences. This connection is an expansion of our emotional repertoire and it makes us far more effective as teachers and leaders who help people claim their greatness.

Approve of Yourself

Bill George, professor at Harvard Business School, former chairman and CEO of Medtronic, and author of *True North: Discover Your Authentic Leadership*, says, "The key to self-acceptance is to love yourself unconditionally." He reminds us that this means acknowledging and accepting our strengths and weaknesses. He further offers, "Loving yourself unconditionally requires self-compassion." It is "that level of self-compassion [that] enables you to get to the source of your True North and to accept yourself as you are."[6] It also is the first level of being able to connect authentically with others, to respect and trust them, to learn from them and empower them, and to support and challenge them.[7]

The statement "I approve of myself" is simple but powerful. It is a statement of self-acceptance. I often ask my students to say it three times before we start learning or applying rigorous material. When we acknowledge fundamental approval of ourselves, we are more accepting of our mistakes as well as our successes. Teachers benefit from self-acceptance, too. So, before you teach a session, *you* might want to say "I approve of myself" five times. As you increase approval of yourself, others will increase approval of themselves, too. Also, when working with learners who are acting out or having difficulty, self-acceptance makes it possible for you to focus not on yourself but on the learners and how you can help them.

Practice Self-Care

Self-care is all too often the last concern of highly challenged, busy people with enormous responsibilities. It is, however, an important priority. If you are not healthy, restored, and resilient on a regular basis, you will not be able to be present, connect, inspire, or engage as effectively as you want. Caring for yourself enables you to put forward your very best self when you teach.

This is important. Think about it: What do you need so that you can do a better job of taking care of yourself? Perhaps you need to get more sleep, sit down when you eat instead of grabbing something on the go, take a walk in nature, go on mini-vacations, absorb doses of regular inspiration, spend quiet time with family, or reflect on more feedback from valued sources. What do you do to connect and care for yourself or to improve your relationships with others while building your practice as a teacher? How do you inspire yourself or seek inspiration from others to stay fresh and keep learning, growing, and developing?

Take Building Excellence
Assessment Now:
See Resource A.

This would be a great time to take an amazing assessment donated to this book from PCI Learn (www. learningstyles.net) called The Building Excellence Profile. See Resource A in the back of the book to access this valuable and extremely educative assessment.

Value Learners and Invest in Success

Everything you do needs to show that you value your learners, care about them, and believe in their success. This mindset opens them to learning. They feel your caring deeply, and it influences them at a profound level. You can demonstrate that you value them by doing small things like greeting them, remembering and calling them by their name, or reiterating something they told you. You can also show you value them by starting your sessions on time and jumping right in to engage them. All of these things show them that they are important and that there are good, solid reasons for being there. Time is a precious commodity; let learners know that you value their time, their commitment, and their interest in your offering. Maintain this mindset as you craft your content, apply the learning design, and personalize the details. This even applies to scheduling breaks and paying attention to small things such as providing energizing snacks and meals. Most importantly, you communicate your respect by making this learning purposeful and meaningful to the learner. Let's peek into two fictional learners' experiences in two different workshops on the same day.

A Tale of Two Classrooms

Nicole, a participant in a leadership development workshop, wakes up extra early so she can take her dog for a walk and still get to her office to print some documents and pick up an important file. She zooms into class one minute before start time. Nicole looks around the room, finds a tent placard with her name on it and a workbook on the table, and sits down. The speaker, standing at a podium in front of the room, welcomes everyone and facilitates introductions around the room for 20 to 30 minutes. Nicole is thinking, "Why did I rush? I could have slept 15 more minutes and squeezed fresh juice. I could have gotten so much more done back at the office." When introductions end, the facilitator shows the first PowerPoint slide with outcomes for the day and dives into a presentation of content. She lectures for 20 to 30 minutes, barely slows down to ask if there are any questions, then speeds right back into her talk. Participants listen, go through the workbook, break for lunch, listen to a little more PowerPoint lecture, watch a video or two, and then zoom back to the office to catch up on e-mail.

Charlie, a participant in a leadership development workshop, wakes up extra early so he can have a cup of coffee and take his daughters to daycare before dashing to the office to check on a couple of work-related issues, pick up a file he requested from his assistant, and grab his pre-work assignment. He makes it to class with a minute or two to spare. As he approaches the room, he hears soft music, and when he gets to the door, the teacher is there to welcome him. He extends his hand, thanks Charlie for coming, asks him about his job, and suggests that Charlie choose a place to sit that feels most comfortable. Charlie settles in. The teacher offers a quick overview of the workshop, then challenges the group with a relevant, provocative question: "Does the world need leaders?" When the participants say, "Yes," the facilitator says, "What are you hoping for as you say 'yes'?" He then asks participants to brainstorm independently, then take turns writing their top ideas on flip charts placed around the room. When everyone is done, the teacher asks each person to introduce himself and share his brilliant thoughts. The sharing of those thoughts leads to an introduction of the high-impact agenda and outcomes for the day.

Which room would you rather be in? Even though Nicole's class might feel more familiar and typical, Charlie's class promises to be a better use of your time and, frankly, feels more appealing. In addition to getting everyone actively involved right away, Charlie's teacher does many things to show consideration for his learners, to communicate that they are important, and to make them feel engaged. The music is a helpful tool for bringing down the early morning stress level and transitioning into the learning environment. By standing in the doorway, Charlie's teacher makes it clear that he wants to connect with everyone personally. When you are teaching or training, greeting people at the door is a great opportunity to find out why each learner is taking your class and what is important to that person. This is not just idle conversation; it is vital information for you to keep in mind and use to make your prepared content meaningful and to engage learners who might need a little special attention. Taking the time to connect personally is a valuable way of showing that this learning event is about the learner, that you care, and that you want the experience to be meaningful to each individual. Even a small thing like letting participants choose their own seat can make a big difference. It may seem minor, but it is an act that gives the learner power. Feeling that

> People don't care how much you know until they know how much you care.

we have power is a huge motivating factor in making the effort to learn.

Let your learners know that you value them, their time, and their commitment to being there by getting them involved early in relevant work and by focusing on them. Saying it is one thing; doing it is another.

REFLECTION: Exercise

THINK BACK/THINK AHEAD

- Think of the last class/meeting you attended that engaged you immediately. What did the manager or teacher do to fire you up?

- What class/meeting are you about to lead? How could you energize, focus, and engage people early on?

Know Your Learners

Who are your learners? What do they bring to the table? What do they know that you don't? How are you connecting with them based on what you know about them and what they need and want personally and professionally? What inspires and drives them? What are their goals? What is their passion and purpose? What transformation do they want to take place? What do they have to do to learn and put the learning into practice? There is no better way to know your learners than to ask them questions and listen to their ideas throughout the learning event. You can do this during formal and informal connections or through a designed activity or a spontaneous moment at the beverage table.

Leverage the Power of Stories

Tell your stories. It will help people remember important concepts. Recently, I went to hear Kevin Freiberg speak on leadership. Kevin is a coach, speaker, and coauthor with his wife, Jackie, of three best-sellers, including *Boom! 7 Choices for Blowing the Doors Off Business-As-Usual.* One of Kevin's key points in his talk was that it is important to act on your values. I might not have remembered that point if Kevin hadn't told a moving personal story about why he made the decision to do less traveling and stay home and do more writing. Kevin shared that he was standing at the door of his house with his suitcase, saying good-bye to his family, when his son looked up at him and said, "Dad, if you value your family, why are you always leaving?" *That* I remember! And because I remember that story, I also remember to live my stated value of the importance of my family.

Encourage participants to tell their stories, to talk about what is important to them, to open themselves up to learning. Create an environment that feels safe and builds trust. Listen to their stories. Build in exercises and time for learners to do the talking, sharing, and teaching. Listening is one of the most important skills for teachers to develop.

Connect Learners to Build a Community of Practice

Kevin Small, President of ResultSource, a leader in book marketing, is one of my favorite people. I call Kevin "The Great Connector" because he really is. He really is the results source! He has helped authors such as John Maxwell, Chip and Dan Heath, Marcus Buckingham, Ken Blanchard, Keith Ferrazzi, and others make their books best-sellers, which helped them achieve other goals. When you are with Kevin and he introduces you to someone, he has an amazing ability to call attention to the strengths and talents of both of you, to make you feel that you are uniquely special and that there will be a magical synergy from this connection that will help you both. As a teacher, you can leverage the impact of connections in your learning situations by showcasing or calling out the uniqueness and talents of all participants and by connecting them to each other. You can help people see that to achieve their life's purpose they need others with talents, knowledge, and connections that are different from their own.

Be Flexible

Great teachers are connected to what is going on around them and flexible while still being purposeful. Although you plan, sometimes you have to be willing to change what you are doing. Once I was working with managers at a large banking organization in the throes of a buyout. The announcement of the buyout came at the beginning of a two-day session I was teaching. Naturally, everyone was concerned with what the buyout was going to mean personally and professionally. While I had been planning to teach participants how to work with their direct reports, in view of the announcement I knew I had to change the focus of my content. Instead, I taught my participants how to make sure they got what they needed in their new positions, and they were right there with me. This willingness to be flexible validated their concerns, helped me connect to them authentically, and made the topic and skills relevant to them.

Last summer, I facilitated a leadership initiative for a branch of the U.S. military. I noticed that one participant seemed particularly distracted and disengaged. He asked to speak to me during a break. I learned that not only had he lost a number of friends in Iraq, but also his wife at home was gravely ill. He confessed that he was trying to do his best to listen and participate, but it was difficult. After listening to his story, I realized it was likely that many other participants were similarly preoccupied. I subtly changed the way I taught the rest of the workshop. By tweaking my language to acknowledge and appreciate the life and death situations this soldier was trying to come to terms with, allowing more time for reflection, and creating respectful ways to connect him with others in the class, I made it more meaningful for him and others to be there.

Read the Room

Everything you do as a teacher can open learners to their own brilliance or it can do the opposite—stifle it. Your demeanor, facial expressions, words, tone, body language, and energy all send messages that can either open people up or shut them down. You can see it as you look around the room. Do you see smiles and sparkling eyes, intent expressions eager for learning? Are people sitting up, leaning forward, maybe on the edge of their seats? Or are they frowning, slumping, checking the time, squirming, and uncomfortable? Do you see joy and enthusiasm? Do you hear the noise of many interacting voices working out solutions and supporting each other, and the quiet of creative energy-exploring possibilities? If so, you will know that you are inspiring the desired outcome, your energy is infectious, and your minute-by-minute choices are paying off. If not, you probably need to change things up. This might mean changing the energy in the room by giving everyone a chance to physically get up and move around. Or maybe you need to interject a little humor or give clearer direction.

Create a Safe Place

For an optimal learning environment, it is imperative to create a protected space where people feel comfortable opening up and grappling with tough concepts. When they feel emotionally safe, they will feel that it is okay to show not just what they do know, but also what they don't know, which will make them more open to learning. As people really believe you care, they will engage at a higher level, and they will rise to meet your expectations.

One way to do this is to show your own vulnerability—to be open about your own mistakes. When teaching how to facilitate virtually, I always tell stories of a wide range of funny mistakes that I made early in my teaching career. This helps people laugh and relax as they see that I have lived and learned by making mistakes.

Be conscious of the language you use to respond to questions or to incorrect answers. Always give learners the opening to try again, to work a little harder to make a connection. Do as much as you can to facilitate their aha moments and to help them be smart.

Joining participants by being with them in the room rather than setting yourself apart is a great way to engender a feeling of safety. This might mean you sit down with them to be part of an exercise, walk around the room as you talk rather than standing behind a podium, and notice if you tend to speak to one side of the room more than another, unconsciously making the people on the other side feel left out. When learners know they are safe, it frees the whole brain and body to learn rather than expending energy worrying or feeling threatened by what the teacher might say or do.

> It's not about how smart they are; it's about *how* they are smart.

When you build safety or support for learning into the framework of your learning design, you and everyone else model it. A former student of mine, Gregg, teaches business writing at the college level and in corporate learning environments. No matter where he is teaching or who the participants are, the defining principles and framework for creating a respectful, trusting, learner-supportive writing community are the same.

Inspired by an objective or a writing craft skill, Gregg's learners participate in a meticulously structured class. His warm-up exercise is designed to make everyone feel competent right away. Many people may feel vulnerable and may be afraid of writing. They think they aren't good enough, and they don't want to be seen as incompetent in such a concrete way. (Does anyone?) The first exercise opens everyone up, makes them feel safe, and helps them connect with what they do know. After this exercise, when they are feeling more confident, they write. Then, when everyone is finished, anyone who chooses to do so reads his or her work aloud. Gregg explains that this part is just as important as the writing. Each reading is followed by feedback, so each participant is responsible for listening authentically. During feedback, it is the job of the students to provide two very important elements: appreciation and positive comments. Gregg tells participants that they can always say, "Thank you for that." He encourages this by modeling it himself for every reader. He models positive feedback by identifying specific words, phrases, or sentences he likes or thinks of as memorable. He also models very specific positive comments, such as "You got your point across quickly and clearly," or "I felt the importance of your request," or "I liked the way you directly asked your team for support." He is clear about zero tolerance for negative comments and criticism. Gregg believes that focusing the learners' attention on the positive things they do engenders more of that skilled behavior. In some settings he facilitates rounds of feedback in response to the question "What could be improved?" The session always ends with what Gregg calls "excessive gratitude" (what I call celebration). He thanks them for their generous mutual support, reminds them of their hard work, and lauds them for bringing out the best in themselves and others.

It is through the vehicle of this clear framework and its ground rules that Gregg creates a safe place—an open learning environment where everyone is more receptive and can take risks, stretch, and work hard without fear of being shut down. It doesn't take long for his students to take the lead in the learning process—writing, showing appreciation, giving positive feedback, building their strengths, and feeling their brilliance.

Recognize That People Want to Learn

It doesn't take much to facilitate or even revive the natural desire to learn and grow. It does, however, take an incredibly generous and courageous heart, less desire for self-importance and ego satisfaction, and a genuine display of belief in a learner's ability to arrive at the knowledge. Your ability to ask for and ignite people's internal motivation and love of learning leverages years of brain-based and learning research and keeps the energy high for you and your learners.

Even though people crave the opportunity to be smart, unleash their talent, and obtain powerful information and new skills, barriers sometimes stand in the way. We are complex individuals with unique life experiences, hang-ups, and daily worries. We have different learning preferences we often aren't even aware of, and we have past learning experiences that may have turned us off. Learners bring all of that with them to your learning sessions. As you know, there are people who seem to be able to learn any way you share information, and others who seem to be unable to focus, learn, or retain anything. Sometimes, these learners act out in ways that can be challenging. What is important for all of us to realize is that there are myriad reasons for reluctance and skepticism, and there are many effective strategies for dealing with those unique challenges.

Although each learner comes to your session with a different history, it is imperative that you assume they all want to learn. Certainly, some come to new learning opportunities with zeal and confidence. Others come with pessimistic attitudes, old baggage, new stresses, and real pressures. Their struggles, failures, and negative experiences from the past cast a shadow and make them closed to new learning. They may be doubtful and insecure about their success or the value of the experience for many reasons, including their own insecurity about their abilities. Sometimes a teacher can trigger memories, even mental "tapes" of bad experiences that are difficult for the learner to overcome alone. In one of my sessions, when I pulled aside a particularly belligerent woman to ask her what was going on, she thought for a moment, then said that I reminded her of her mother, and she was not going to let me "make her do anything again!" Once the young woman heard herself say that aloud, we laughed, and she was able to put her issue with her mother aside and fully focus on the class.

In another session, I became aware of a man who seemed to be glaring at me for a long while. When I asked him what was going on, he told me he didn't know what to do in the assigned activity. What I was interpreting as anger or reluctance to get involved was actually a feeling of frustration and worry about being held accountable for something he missed. Although I had given some direction and others were working, he felt lost. I hadn't been specific enough for him. He needed more step-by-step instruction. Once I gave it to him and walked him through the first part, he relaxed and stepped into the flow of the lesson. This same young man became one of the people who recorded a testimonial about the power of the content and course at the end of the day!

By the time children reach second grade, many have already learned to doubt their abilities and talents. They've experienced adults who have to be right and who want to win and be superior. This attitude is unproductive and is more about power and ego than learning. Not only does it dampen openness to learning, sometimes it shuts it right down. Learners affected by this approach often do what a turtle does—recess into a protective shell or try to hide or be invisible. They are afraid to stand out for fear of being not good enough. Because of their lack of confidence, they try to figure out what the teacher is looking for rather than think for themselves. Thankfully, there are many great teachers who restore a learner's confidence and who reignite the trust, openness, and the love of learning that many of us safely had in preschool. Great teachers want learners to think and to feel. They make it safe to step out of comfort zones and take the risks necessary to learn. Although some learners display a negative attitude or are rude, angry, uncooperative, or downright resentful about being in class, it usually is to cover up their own insecurity. It is possible to turn all those barriers around and help the learner feel at ease and open to learning.

Assume Positive Intention

Often, people act out and resist learning because of something going on in their lives outside the classroom. They may feel powerless in the face of change, or afraid of making yet another mistake. They may have had a serious fight with a spouse or family member, or they may be worried about losing their job. They may be on a diet, they may have low blood sugar and feel edgy, or perhaps they are worried about making financial ends meet.

It is essential to assume positive intention on the part of every learner. Regardless of the signs a student may be giving you that he or she is closed to learning, you need to believe that, underneath, there is a genuine desire to learn. When a learner's behaviors and intentions are not in sync, you can bring them into alignment by building trust that you sincerely want the learner to be successful, not just in your learning session but also in life. If you communicate this over and over again, the student will eventually believe you and open up.

Help People Be Smart

Whether your learners are talkative, angry, aggressive, inconsiderate, know-it-all, quiet, overly sensitive, or trying to be funny, there are behavior management strategies that might help you. Interestingly, I've found that some of my most challenging learners, if handled with grace, honesty, and sincerity, have become some of my greatest proponents and even lifelong friends. Your best approach is a respectful, honest, caring one. By asking, "Would it be okay if I share something I have noticed?" and really listening to the response, you give that person a voice, and you learn as well as teach.

As you read the following suggestions, remember that your goal is to help everyone be successful and have an optimal learning experience. Since everyone is different, you and your learners will benefit from a diverse repertoire of strategies and approaches.

Some specific types of challenges you might encounter are situations where someone:

- Can't stop talking
- Can't seem to talk
- Tells you everything about themselves
- Name-drops
- Seems apathetic, lazy, bored, or uninterested
- Tells a joke a minute
- Acts stressed
- Seems chemically dependent
- Acts like a know-it-all
- Seems to dislike you before they even know you

I am a firm believer that people are doing the best they can on any given day. Few people wake up and think, "I am going to be a lousy learner and disrupt the class (or meeting) today." The faster we realize that, and truly believe that someone's acting out has nothing to do with us, the faster we go down the learner's path to seek a mutually beneficial solution versus letting someone's behavior disrupt the learning experience. By assuming positive intent and asking yourself, "Why might a rational person be acting this way?" you move to a more productive place—a place of generosity and problem solving.

Being a respectful, sensitive teacher doesn't mean that you have to become everyone's counselor, psychologist, or social worker. However, as I said previously, you will be a stronger, more effective, and likely happier teacher if you choose to work with all learners rather than entering into a contentious battle or ignoring them. To do this, you will want to be aware of your inner judge or critic. Be sure you are reminding yourself that you are okay and that you approve of yourself. If you are positive with yourself, you can engender that behavior with your students.

Address the Cause

Often we assume that we know why someone is doing what we observe, and that may cause us to label the person versus objectively finding out what is going on. People can't read minds. (I get myself into trouble constantly because I forget this and think I can!) The faster you move toward the person and ask him what his observable behavior means, the faster you can address what is wrong. Remember to celebrate individuality and be curious about the person and his world versus being annoyed.

Build Self-Esteem

People who don't like themselves much may have difficulty enjoying and be-ing open to situations that could prove them right. They may have deep fear of not being "good enough," and this fear shows up as some of the behaviors mentioned earlier. They may be approval seekers or perfectionists who are hard on themselves. Their anger and disappointment may show up as a lack of faith in anything that might help them be successful. As you notice them, make them feel important and weave their ideas, answers, and suggestions into the learning session. You can be the one who helps them alter their in-grained belief that they just aren't good enough and helps them realize that they really are okay. Your patience, assumption of positive intention, and con-fidence building can help them relax into the experience so they can hear their own ideas and experience what it is like for someone to notice them be-cause of their gifts. This encourages them to contribute at their highest level.

Open a Trust Fund

Many reasons exist for why a learner acts bored or positions himself as "know-it-all," contrarian, or the resident comedian. Subliminally, this per-son may have a fear of being wrong or looking stupid. They want to know that they can trust you to not make them feel worse than they already feel about themselves and their capabilities, and that it is safe to reveal their truths. To build this trust, support learners by setting them up to win with your great content, models, and materials and by giving directions that are concise and actionable. Another way to ensure a safer learning environ-ment is to stick with them until their response is right and they know they have grasped the new concept. This means you ask them their rationale and help move them to the correct response rather than just moving to another person for the right answer. To build trust, you need to be compe-tent, sincere, and authentic, and validate who they really are.

Create Opportunities for Success

To create a community of learners, give everyone the chance to achieve early success in front of their peers. Sometimes learners hold back for fear of being wrong and looking stupid in front of others. They live a self-fulfilling proph-ecy by living out other people's expectations instead of reaching for their own aspirations. In the past, they may have always gotten away with being "good enough," but subconsciously they know they could do better. You can be the one—the change agent—who breaks their pattern of behavior and empowers them to take greater risks. By using your power as a teacher and starting with simple questions that generate discussion and help learners look intelligent in front of their peers, you can challenge them to tap into their innate brain-power and succeed at more difficult situations that may arise later on.

Focus on What You Can Control

As I've said earlier, learners come to learning sessions with all of their life experiences. Possibly you have heard some of their personal stories and been humbled by the kinds of difficulties they are dealing with. Current events in all aspects of our lives influence attitude and behavior when we're trying to learn. It's important to care, but the fact remains that you can't control what is going on outside your sphere of influence. Trying to do so would be overwhelming and unproductive.

I believe you can help learners who are acting out or preoccupied by focusing on what you *can* control—the immediate learning experience. You can control the flow, content, and learning design. If everyone is distracted and listless, there is a good chance you need to change things up. Try another way of stating what you just said or asking them to do an activity. Get people up to the flip chart or the computers and ask them to generate three questions about what you are teaching. Help them release some of their angst and refocus by taking immediate action. Success breeds success. The faster you show people how much they can learn, the faster they want to learn more.

Be the Visible Patrol

What do you do if you see a police car when you are driving? You check the speedometer, look around you, and make sure you are obeying the laws. Perhaps you slow down, make sure you use your turn signals, and generously let cars change lanes in front of you. You can be a police car in your meeting or class and have the same influence. Without saying anything, you can reengage learners while minimizing disruptive behaviors such as checking smartphones, talking, multitasking, and avoiding the assignment. By moving closer to someone checking e-mail or standing right next to two people not involved in the group activity, you can put them on high alert, and that alone may stop the behavior and reengage the learner(s).

Change Their State

To reduce resistance to learning, sometimes you just have to change what I call a person's "state." Ask people to stand up, stretch, breathe, drink a glass of water, get a snack, listen to a song, or make a subliminal affirmation, such as "I can learn _____."

29

All of these strategies break the wall of emotion and address physical limitations that may be blocking learning. When you fundamentally value the individual and respect where they are in their life at the moment, you empower them to show up as the person they would like to be and help them actualize their greatest potential.

Flip Your Focus

When I went through training to become a counselor, one of my instructors taught me to flip my focus from myself to my patient. This has been a valuable strategy for me that I have remembered and used throughout my career. When I think, "He hates me," I am making his behavior about me. When I get really clear about the essence of my feeling and flip my focus or change my perspective to "He hates himself" or "He seems to be angry— what might have made him hate the world right now?" this shifts my perspective to focusing on the patient, or on my learner. Instead of thinking, "What a pain," I can try to understand what might have made him so angry or why he might hate himself, and I can focus on how to help him understand it so he can move on. This really works. If I say to myself, "She thinks I am not too smart," I am making someone else's behavior about me. If I flip my focus to "She doesn't think she is very smart," I can focus on finding ways to help her believe in her own intelligence.

Another strategy for flipping your focus and changing your perspective to build better relationships and better results comes from the book *You're Never Upset for the Reason You Think* by Paul and Layne Cutright.[8] When you are upset with a learner, you often think it is about them and their behavior. Paul and Layne share that you can take the emotional charge out of the upset by focusing on *your* reactions and figuring out what this person triggered in you. Early in my training career at The Ken Blanchard Companies, I went to Clorox to do a training with a dynamic, highly educated group of brand managers. Just thinking about their Ivy League degrees while flying there made me a bit nervous about whether I was good enough to be teaching them. To overcome my insecurity, I led with my ego, wanting to impress them with how much I knew and to show them how smart *I* was. Needless to say, this alienated them. Thankfully, I realized that *they* weren't the challenge, *I* was. Instead of assuming positive intention on their part, I assumed negative judgment. When I flipped my perspective from "I want them to see me as smart" to "I want them to be smart," I got my ego out of the way and began to listen to just how brilliant they were, and the rest of the session opened up to invite everyone's learning.

Help Learners Find Their Voice

Helping learners feel brilliant and express their unique thoughts is a challenge for even the most talented teacher. Success can depend on a range of incredibly diverse variables that might include what the participant ate that day, what's going on at home or in their minds, their moods, how far behind they are in their work, how satisfied or dissatisfied they are with their job, how stressed or calm they are, how interested they are in your topic, and what's going on in the world.

As you take on the challenge of being an architect of learning, remember that whether your learners are in a meeting, a workshop, or in an online class, people like to feel brilliant. They love to learn, speak knowledgeably about something new, and wrestle with it until it becomes theirs. Brilliant feelings transfer to taking on greater learning risks, exploration, and innovative thinking.

REFLECTION: Review

BRING OUT BRILLIANCE

- Rebalance the Learning Equation: The 70/30 Principle
- Create a Continuous Flow of Connections
- Brilliance Starts with You
  - Know Yourself
  - Connect with Self and Others
  - Approve of Yourself
  - Practice Self-Care
- Value Learners and Invest in Success
  - Know Your Learners
  - Leverage the Power of Stories
  - Connect Learners to Build a Community of Practice
  - Be Flexible

(Continued)

- Read the Room
- Create a Safe Place
- Recognize That People Want to Learn
- Assume Positive Intention
- Help People Be Smart
  - Address the Cause
  - Build Self-Esteem
  - Open a Trust Fund
  - Create Opportunities for Success
  - Focus on What You *Can* Control
  - Be the Visible Patrol
  - Change Their State
  - Flip Your Focus
- Help Learners Find Their Voice

CHAPTER **2**

Craft Content That Sings

When you craft the second component of the Brilliance Learning System, your *Content,* you focus on extreme clarity and activities that build your manageable nuggets of information and on models that integrate key themes.

Thanks to Professor Wilson, I graduated from UC Davis and got my teaching credentials. The first time I taught a full lesson, however, was during one of my education classes. My learners were my classmates and our popular but demanding professor. I wanted to do something that would knock their socks off and demonstrate what I believed, which was that every lesson could inspire a love of learning. I decided to pretend this lesson was the first in a literature program, and I would teach the poem "On Giving" by Kahlil Gibran as an introduction to teaching the short story "The Gift of the Magi" by O. Henry.[1]

I ran off copies of "On Giving" on parchment-like paper and wrapped each one in a package, making them as beautiful as possible. No two were exactly alike. I began the lesson by walking through the aisles with a basket, handing each student one of my gifts. As I offered each one, I smiled and said, "I have a gift for you." I made a mental note that every one of my "students" met my eyes with their own as the gift left my hand and went into theirs. I asked everyone not to open the package yet, but to jot down immediately their first thoughts—words, phrases, or sentences—about the experience of receiving this gift. As I met each of their gazes and my basket emptied, my confidence was building. Then I asked everyone to get into small groups of four or five to share their notes on the gift-receiving experience, and stories about expectations in other gift giving/receiving experiences such as birthday and holiday rituals with their families or others. Someone in each group recorded notes and made a list of common themes. We came together as a whole group again and engaged in an energetic exchange of stories and ideas about how it feels to give and receive, as well as our intentions, expectations, and disappointments. They still hadn't opened the little parcels. Finally, I asked everyone to pick a partner and take turns opening their gifts. While one person opened his or her gift, the other person acted as a witness, noticing and writing down observations. Then I asked the witnesses to share their observations with their partners. At last, we came together as a whole group to read the poem aloud. In small groups again, the students discussed the ideas in the poem. I asked them to think about their ideas in relationship to their personal experiences and to share memorable stories. The room was noisy with lively discussion, and I was excited. In the end, we came together as a whole group to share the great ideas that emerged.

The gift I received was the experience that if I deliver my content using a learning design that actively involves the learners, connects them to their own knowledge and experience, includes novel activities, and gives them the space to arrive at the learning, I can trust that *the important concepts I want students to come away with will emerge from them, rather than from me.* Everything I hoped to teach and more bubbled up from the students that day. I didn't have to *tell* them; they *discovered* the key ideas. It was my job and my responsibility to focus and inspire them to do the work, create the groundwork and the environment, and give it all a meaningful context. I realized that no matter how rich and valuable my content, it meant nothing if I didn't capture the interest of my students, make it meaningful, and help them facilitate their own brilliance.

From that very first lesson, I worked hard to create an interactive, engaged style of teaching that has proven successful throughout the years across a range of audiences and subjects. In this chapter, I share what I have discovered to be the most salient strategies when crafting content that really sings, connects to learners, and unlocks brilliance.

Craft content that sings.

Invite Learners to Experience the Content

My first lesson would have fallen flat and left everyone uninterested and bored if I hadn't focused on the learners. I involved and connected them in meaningful ways to the main ideas. Through engagement, I captured their attention, provoked their curiosity, and pushed them to think differently and more expansively. I took the abstract idea of a "gift" and made it concrete. It had physicality, which connected the students to the physical experience of giving and receiving. Their sensory memory in connection with my questions and activities related them to other experiences. The students could draw from their own personal experiences and listen and learn from each other. We began with something easy and unthreatening and then stretched into more expansive thinking, which enticed them to go deeper. Through the variety of activities, students focused on themselves and worked collaboratively as they learned from others. We varied activities, working together in pairs, in small groups, and as a whole class. The concepts became as malleable and animated as our discussions. All of this variety got everyone involved— connecting, speaking, listening, sharing, learning—and the entire lesson prepared them for the more challenging content coming up.

35

Connect Abstract Concepts through Concrete Examples

One way I am often confused when listening to speakers is when I can't seem to form a picture of what they are describing. I see their mouths move, but I just don't *get* what they are saying. You can help learners like me by including concrete examples when possible in your content. When you take an abstract idea and make it meaningful and usable for the learner, you are making that learning more accessible. To do so, you want to link it to a common experience, knowledge, or previous understanding.

Let's say, for example, you were teaching someone how the ear works, and you wanted that person to understand the concept of a decibel. You might ask, "Have you ever put a headset on and wondered where the sound was coming from?" Interesting question, isn't it? At the least, most of your learners probably would nod or register some expression that this is a question worth considering. On the other hand, what if you said, "A decibel is a unit of relative loudness, electric voltage, or current equal to 10 times the common logarithm of the ratio of two readings"? Although that very detailed information is accurate, it likely is an overload of facts that would whiz right through people's brains. There isn't a handhold or foothold to grasp to understand all that. A different question to further a more concrete connection might be, "If you are listening to beautiful music, what's happening that makes it possible for you to hear it?" Your provocative question links the concept of a decibel to a concrete experience that pretty much everyone has had.

To help your learners grasp your content, you want to frame it in a context they know and understand so that they can use that context to hook new information onto the old. A great way to do this is to create a friendly model, method, system, or framework.

Design Your Content and Create Your Model

A client called one time because his organization was losing a high percentage of people within the first year and he thought it was possible they weren't hiring the right people. He wanted me to do a presentation on how to select great people. After interviewing many people in the organization, I concluded that it was not just a selection issue; it was a selection and development issue. I interviewed subject matter experts, read everything I could get my hands on, wrote notes on all the key messages, sorted them by themes, and then created a model around these groups of core topics. I called this structure the THRIVE model, since the purpose was to teach people in organizations how to hire people who would "thrive" or be successful. The THRIVE Model contained the key steps I wanted people to learn.

The THRIVE Model

Hire People Who THRIVE. The people who . . .

Title:	Know the actual job they will be doing and how it impacts overall business results.
Heart:	Have the attitude critical to success in this job.
Results:	Know the measurable results that they will be held accountable for (what actions need to be taken).
Important skills:	Currently, or will ultimately, have the performance and technical skills that will enable them to achieve desired results.
Values:	Are in sync with your organization's values, thus creating synergy.
Excellence:	Have a proven track record of overcoming obstacles and achieving excellence in their job.

A model is a framework to help people make sense of new ideas. It also helps you clarify key concepts to yourself and to your learners. You can develop a model, a framework, a methodology, or a system—whatever works for your content to make the learning easier *and* more actionable. In a little while, we will walk through the ENGAGE Model, the learning design I created for the Brilliance Learning System that you can use, as I do, to design and teach any topic. Your goal, though, is to make a model or framework that is specific to your topic.

Develop a Job Aid or One-Page Synthesis

Once you have created a model, framework, or method, it is always helpful to develop a job aid—a concise, usable tool with key concepts. This tool helps you and your learners synthesize the concepts. It can be as practical as a one-page checklist or a business card–sized synopsis. You and your learners will find that it is a learning power tool. Figure 2.1 shows the job

Title	• What is the actual job? • How does it link to business results? • What are the key responsibility areas?
Heart	• What attitudes will make them thrive?
Results	• What measurable results will they be held accountable for?
Important skills	• Can they achieve results? • What technical and performance skills are needed?
Values	• Will they fit with our culture and values?
Excellence	• What is one goal for this person to be able to achieve?

Figure 2.1. Job Aid for the THRIVE Model for Hiring

aid I created for the THRIVE Model. Remember, I wanted this tool to help people remember the steps for hiring people who will thrive and feel they are successful.

Craft Your Content—Ideas for Consideration

You bring your knowledge and expertise to the content. In this chapter and in subsequent chapters outlining the ENGAGE Model, your outcome is to craft your content so that it is exciting, understandable, meaningful, and applicable to learners.

Think out loud now about your content and how you can make it sing. What do you need to be mindful of as you craft it? Below is an initial list for your consideration. Make some notes alongside it or in a notebook. Start brainstorming. How can you apply these characteristics to your content?

❑ Make content clear, concise, and accessible.

❑ Focus your content on learner needs.

❑ Articulate your core message and concepts.

❑ State your desired outcome/result explicitly.

❑ Use concrete examples to support clarity and learning.

❑ Connect to learners' knowledge and experience.

❏ Present content in small chunks or building blocks.

❏ Create a meaningful model and job aid that is a powerful tool for learning.

❏ Plan abundant opportunities for varied, meaningful, interactive exercises.

❏ Ensure your purpose is clear and relevant to the learners' objectives.

❏ Ask yourself what you want learners to know—become adept at asking tough questions, use these questions to drill down, and have learners work harder to deepen understanding and application.

❏ Design a model and methodology that ensures learners have ample opportunity for discovery through exploration.

❏ Be knowledgeable of what other people in your field are saying and contributing.

Clarify Your Message: Release Energy

My husband, Rick, is the Director of the California Chaparral Institute. One day, he came home elated after giving a talk to a group of distinguished scientists. Although he had been a little nervous the night before, he said that it turned out to be his best speech ever. He credited the quality of his talk to his clarity. As part of his preparation, he practiced articulating his message out loud with me to make sure that he was extremely clear.

Clear content energizes and focuses the brain on a challenging target. What is the core message of your content? What do you want people to learn? Can you articulate your core message and objectives? Can you say them and write them clearly in one or two sentences? If a reporter were interviewing you for a five-minute spot or a one-paragraph article, how would you respond to the following questions: What is your program about? What are the key concepts? What do you want people to walk away with from your program? And, if there is still time in the interview, could you explain in what ways your program will impact or change their lives?

> Clear content gives the brain a challenging target.

To spark your clarity, here are a few more questions: How do you hope that learners will take your message and content into their lives? What do you really want people to know? What do you want them to be able to do? What do you want them to believe? Most people think that because an idea is in their mind, they will be able to access it, say it, and write it clearly, but that's usually not the case. Clarity takes practice.

Exercise: Clarity

Let's practice being clear about the core message of our content. Think of a specific topic or learning event now. What do you want to teach? What is your core message? Try to articulate it. Say it aloud. Write it down. Over the course of a few days or a week, refine it. If you need some help getting started, you might try doing an Internet search on your topic or going to a library or bookstore to see how others frame their message. Construct your message using language that feels true to you. Use a dictionary and thesaurus as well as other references to find accurate language. Then ask a friend, colleague, or family member to listen and give you feedback on your clarity. Record it and listen. Take all the feedback you can get to clarify your message, to make it meaningful and powerful.

> Ask a friend, colleague, or family member to listen and give you feedback on your clarity.

Shift Beliefs and Break Through Barriers

Once you have a clear message, focus on the beliefs you would like participants to adopt so they can absorb the new content. My good friend and editor, Margie, a teacher/instructional designer and author living in Minnesota, wrote to me about an interesting speaking engagement she'd had. She was invited to speak to the secondary school faculties of a school district embarking on a community-wide Sustained Silent Reading (SSR) program. Wanting as much background information as possible, she asked when and how the SSR program would be implemented, and her contact said it would take place during class time and study halls. No one had designed a plan. Each teacher was pretty much on his own.

The goal in SSR is to give every student designated time every day to experience silent reading so that it becomes a habit or practice. My friend organized ideas for initiating and maintaining the reading program. She pulled together lists of resources and suggestions for using them, and she included scripts for interacting with the students, noticing the positive, giving rewarding feedback, and celebrating the SSR practice. This was easy for her, and it was important: these would be the tools and strategies the teachers hoped to get from her to make their job easier. Margie was smart enough to know that for the program to be successful, every member of the faculty and staff would have to own it, believe in it, and become genuinely involved. Margie prepared an exercise around beliefs, thoughts, and expectations to frame her talk. It's a good thing she was so insightful. On the morning she was giving her talk, she read in the newspaper that the voters in that school district had voted down a referendum for additional funding for education. Not a good omen. It occurred to her that the teachers would be even more negative than she suspected. They were being asked to take on another responsibility and squeeze yet another program into their already packed schedules, with no additional resources. She was now even more certain that her biggest challenge of the day would be turning around the beliefs of the teachers. And yet she knew this was essential if the teachers were going to turn around the beliefs of the students.

As soon as she was introduced, Margie began walking through the rows of seats with sheets of paper and pencils. As she walked, she talked. "Please join me in an experiment. I'd like you to write down a list of your beliefs, thoughts, and expectations about the Sustained Silent Reading program being instituted in your schools this term." She told everyone to write "I" statements: I believe . . . I think . . . I expect . . . And she assured them that their statements would remain confidential. When they were finished, she asked them to place their list on their seat and sit on it. Margie gave her talk. She suggested that the principals, vice principals, librarians, coaches, science teachers—and anyone else who could do it—start book clubs that met for 20 minutes during lunch periods or before or after school. She asked how many planned to read during the SSR sessions they would be facilitating. Not one hand went up. From their expressions, she read that this was not something they'd considered, but Margie could see it was a belief-shifter for some. She recommended that everyone read, that they model the behavior they expected from the students, and maybe even have a small library of materials on hand: a section of the newspaper, a book about the supernatural, short stories, a graphic novel, a book on how to fix stuff, a memoir or biography, and special interest magazines on music, food, sports, travel, science, movies, or entertainment. She opened her proverbial toolbox and emptied it, giving them everything she could within the limits of her time to help them succeed. She prodded them to share their own ideas and feelings about the importance of reading in their lives. She asked, "What is your favorite book and why?" Pretty soon there was an exchange she hoped would carry over after she left.

> What you *do* lasts longer in the mind of the student than what you *say*.

With less than 10 minutes to go, Margie walked through the room again, handed out fresh sheets of paper and pencils, and asked everyone to write their beliefs, thoughts, and expectations, using "I" statements just as they did earlier. She noticed that the principal was writing his list. There were some people who were less than enthusiastic, but she had definitely felt the energy in the room shift during her talk. She saw eyes sparkling, heard eagerness in voices, fielded a lot of good questions, and watched as many sat straighter on the edges of their seats and took notes. She knew that most were onboard and excited now about being involved in the SSR program, but she wanted them to get it—to recognize the belief shift that had taken place. She asked people to compare the list they were sitting on with the second list they wrote at the end. She gave them a minute or two for the noticeable shift to sink in. Then she asked people to articulate what they were walking away with—to name one idea they were going to try. When she finished, many faculty members smiled and thanked her, and she could feel their sincere gratitude. The principal of the high school made a point of telling her he had already selected the first title for his book club.

Hyrum Smith, in his book *What Matters Most,*[2] taught me the concept of a "belief window." In one of my greatest aha moments, I learned that to permanently change behavior, one has to change the beliefs below the surface— the beliefs or window we look through to judge or drive current behavior. Otherwise, the change will be temporary. As a teacher, this is pivotal to your success.

At the time I learned about the belief window, I was trying to eat healthier foods. With all my traveling, I was less successful than I wanted to be. When I analyzed the belief that drove my behavior to get a Tasty Turkey Bagel Sandwich (yum) versus a chicken salad at Einstein Bros. Bagels, I realized that my current belief was "If I work hard, I need to eat more to sustain my energy." I realized that my behavior followed or was aligned with that belief. My reframed belief, "Eating healthy gives me greater energy," has inspired me to select many more salads!

Beliefs drive behavior that results in change over time. If you target a behavior without examining and changing an underlying belief, you run the risk of igniting a short-term change rather than a more enduring one. So let's think for a minute about your core message. What beliefs do you want people to adopt so they will embrace the new content? What do you want your learners to believe so they can change their behavior?

> What beliefs do you want people to adopt so they will embrace the new content?

When teaching the new behaviors associated with topics such as leadership, service, communication, and trust, you want learners to address their own beliefs and, if necessary, shift them. They may not be aware of them or that they are barriers to moving forward. As you think about your content, consider the beliefs that help people embody and practice the new learning, as well as those beliefs that stand in the way.

A belief I often want to shift in the minds of managers when I teach leadership and management is "If I give someone clear direction, I'll be perceived as a micromanager." This belief often creates confusion and disappointment for both manager and those being managed. It can set people up for failure instead of success. Why? When people are new to a job or an organization, they may have the skills for the job, but they don't know the specific policies, procedures, and best practices for that organization. Managers can help their staff be successful and live up to expectations of great success by teaching people how to get things done "around here." Without training, mentoring, or modeling, success is left to chance. This lack of clear direction often is due to the prevalent managerial belief "If I give someone clear direction, I'll be perceived as a micromanager." To support the success of their staff, the belief-shift I want managers and leaders to hold is: "People crave direction when first learning. Giving clear direction supports success." And a belief I would want learners to adopt is: "I add value by learning from the expertise of others." Think about concrete examples of fast-held beliefs people may have in relation to your content, and consider how to reframe those beliefs to help them be successful.

Deep Practice Changes Brain Chemistry

In the book *The Talent Code,*[3] Daniel Coyle explains that myelin, an insulating coating that wraps neural connections, increases through deep practice. The more we do something, the more myelin wraps or coils around the neural connection, forming a sheath—picture a fruit roll-up. Coyle tells us that the work of Dr. R. Douglas Fields, director of the Laboratory of Developmental Neurobiology at the National Institutes of Health in Bethesda, Maryland, shows that myelin only wraps one way—and it doesn't unwrap. So what does this mean for those of us who are trying to change behavior with our new content? It means that any behavior, life practice, or belief that people have maintained for a long period of time is extremely resistant to change, and that these likely are so deeply embedded that they will always be there. *To change existing beliefs and practices, we have to help learners to create new, even stronger neural connections to new patterns of behavior.* Very often, the reason we aren't unleashing greatness and actually helping people exhibit new behaviors is because the old behaviors have a stronger connection. They override the new belief or behavior.

This awareness has huge implications for learning and how we teach. To teach new ideas and patterns of behavior requires a clear target, shifts in beliefs, and shifts in how we teach. It requires a rebalancing of the learning equation.

REFLECTION: Review

CHARACTERISTICS OF LEARNER-CENTERED CONTENT AND TEACHING

- Extreme clarity around core message, concepts, and objectives heightens the brain's natural tendencies to problem solve and discover aha moments.

- The one who is doing the talking is doing the learning, so get learners talking about your content early.

- Active involvement with concepts versus passive listening enhances learning.

- If your content is clear so that people can teach it to each other, every time they teach it, they triple their retention of information.

- Interactivity means interacting with content, thus deepening retention.

- Increasing the rigor and experiencing the deep aha moments enhances the learning.

- Stories that link to your ideas tap into the emotion zone of the brain, which stimulates memory.

- Building in choice empowers learners; empowered learners work harder.

- Asking for brilliance, being audacious, and making learners work hard with your clear content is your responsibility, as is celebrating and making the accomplishments meaningful along the way.

- The more clear, rigorous practice the learner does with your content, the more automatic and natural it will be to use that content.

Model Creation
DO-IT-YOURSELF TEMPLATE

1 What is (are) your big idea(s)?

_____
_____
_____

2 What do you want people to be able to do when they are done learning your content?

_____
_____
_____
_____
_____
_____
_____
_____
_____
_____
_____
_____
_____

3 What are the 3 to 6 key themes, main ideas, principles, parts, skills, or behaviors that will enable people to do step 2?

_____
_____
_____
_____
_____

4 From your themes (step 3), what words trigger your big idea (step 1)?

_____, _____, _____
_____, _____, _____.

Choose words to put in boxes below and chronologically create steps from your key concepts.

Words   **Steps**

[_____]   _____

[_____]   _____

[_____]   _____

[_____]   _____

[_____]   _____

[_____]   _____

[_____]   _____

CHAPTER **3**

The ENGAGE Model: An Overview

The ENGAGE Model represents the third component of the Brilliance Learning System that teachers (*who*) can use to create a learning design to teach their content (*what*). Its purpose is to immerse or "engage" learners actively with the new information and concepts to unleash their brilliance over time and to inspire so much passion about their learning that they walk away zealous about putting it into practice and teaching it to others. ENGAGE is about designing learning that drives outcomes and gets people to commit to action (see Figure 3.1).

Cross the Bridge to Learning

You are now at the bridge that leads to the ENGAGE Model, which will show you *how* to structure the total learning experience to achieve your objectives and create an optimal experience for your learners. This chapter gives you a preview of coming attractions. You will see how the six steps in the model fit together to create a powerful, multidimensional structure—the instructional design you can use to inspire deep understanding and

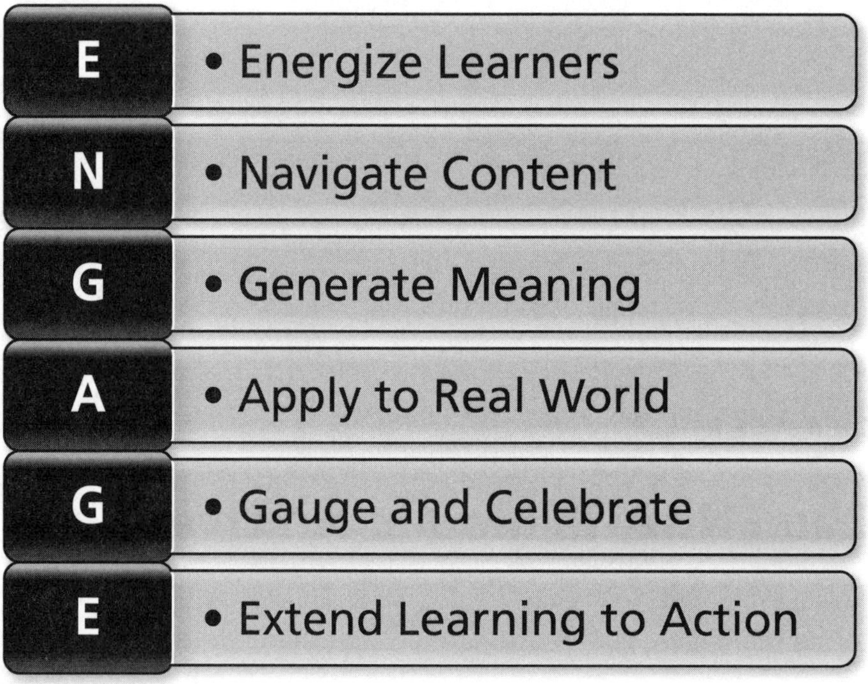

E	• Energize Learners
N	• Navigate Content
G	• Generate Meaning
A	• Apply to Real World
G	• Gauge and Celebrate
E	• Extend Learning to Action

Figure 3.1.   The ENGAGE Model

meaning for your learners to enable them to integrate their new knowledge into their lives and work.

When I went through Coach Certification at New Ventures West Coaching in San Francisco, the program was implemented with precision and care. Before I started the course, I received (*Energize Learners*) a clear, passionate overview of the total program along with testimonials, a series of questions to answer, books to review, references to read, and step-by-step instructions for how to successfully prepare for my first face-to-face session. Upon arriving at my first of four full-day sessions, I was quickly (*Navigate Content*) challenged, educated, inspired, and eager to make this a part of my life's practices. I watched and discussed (*Generate Meaning*) the amazing power of coaching, dissected what those phenomenal coaches did, rigorously practiced each discrete skill with other students in the class, and received in-between session work. The learning over time helped my coaching skills to emerge and integrate with what I knew to be true, so when it was time to (*Apply to Real World*) do our practicum with three new coaching clients, I had the tools and support to be successful. Our celebration of learning (*Gauge and Celebrate*), coaching a stranger in a live situation in front of the panel of experts, solidified all I had learned and enabled me to move forward with my dream of helping people claim their greatness. The learning continues to this day (*Extend the Learning to Action*), with each new development stage of my life helping me take in greater depth of knowledge and application through roundtable discussions, book study groups, virtual trainings, and reunion weekends. In short, I developed a new competence, made lifelong friends, and was thoroughly connected, inspired, and engaged throughout. This carefully designed coaching program is a great example of the six-step ENGAGE Model.

Why six steps instead of two? Really learning to do something new is rigorous. These six steps were mindfully formulated based on what we have learned and what I have personally experienced through my 35 years of teaching. Change, which is learning, has to build over time. The six steps of the ENGAGE Model provide the time and the essential practice to achieve learning that lasts and gets results. Recent discoveries in neuroscience and learning behavior tell us that in order to learn something or change an ingrained behavior, we have to override a preexisting behavior with a stronger, newer one. For a new behavior to become automatic, *that* takes time and practice.[1] Think about how many times you flip on a light switch for a burnt-out bulb that you've been meaning to replace for four months. Ten times? Twenty times? A month? Three months? Maybe longer? Your pattern of flipping on the light when you go into your closet is so deeply ingrained it is really hard to change it. You have to lay down a new neural connection that is more deeply ingrained so that your automatic behavior remembers the bulb is burnt out. (Of course, you might want to replace the bulb sooner!) And that will only happen through rigorous, repeated practice that takes place over time.

The six steps of the ENGAGE Model provide that necessary practice over time that people need in order to embrace the behaviors you want them to learn, and it is, as I said, multidimensional. It taps into our aliveness, our energy. It unites our emotional, mental, and physical being, which is why people feel so "engaged," and why they often feel uplifted, excited, "energized," even transformed, as if something has moved in them or they have accessed more of themselves. The ENGAGE Model brings out the best—the brilliance—in teachers and learners by tapping into our energy source, giving it release, then nourishing, sustaining, and releasing it over and over again through the continuous cycle of connecting, inspiring, and engaging. The six steps create a positive emotional state that makes learners open to learning new information. That openness makes the learner willing to do the hard work and necessary practice. That hard work and practice inspires an eagerness to implement and apply the learning in their lives, and fosters a desire to seek out other people, build a community, share the learning, and explore and expand possibilities, which multiplies the learning exponentially. ENGAGE creates learning that brings you closer to the life you are seeking, to your immediate goals and greater aspirations, and maybe to aspirations you weren't even aware you had.

ENGAGE: Best Practices

Remember Nicole and Charlie, our fictional learners in two different leadership workshops in Chapter 2? Nicole's workshop was the familiar but unrewarding "sit 'n' get" model. It's likely that Nicole's learning experience didn't change much in her life. Charlie's workshop was a completely different experience. From the music he heard while walking toward the room and his teacher's greeting in the doorway to the challenging question that kicked off learning and the brainstorming that followed, Charlie felt *engaged*. In Charlie's workshop, there was a huge mutual investment in bringing out Charlie's brilliance and sending him out into the world feeling empowered to change his life by using his knowledge. Charlie was in a workshop based on the Brilliance Learning System and the ENGAGE Model. Step by step, Charlie's teacher built his instructional design and implemented it in Charlie's workshop where it all came to life by incorporating the following best practices as building blocks:

- Capture the attention and align the learning with the deep interest of the learners.
- Fill the learning time with interactive skill-building activities so the learner can handle, feel, massage, use, and apply the new learning.
- Inspire learners to drill down to make the connections they need to deepen understanding, make the knowledge their own, and apply it in their own way.
- Consider the variety of ways people learn best and incorporate a multisensory approach to learning the content that includes novelty, creativity, and playfulness.
- Incorporate the practice of reflecting and stretching the learners' minds by thinking differently from the way they normally do.
- Create an environment in which people feel safe to practice, make mistakes, take risks, and learn.
- Make people feel smart throughout the process by giving them consistent encouragement and useful, authentic affirmations.

Incorporate a multisensory approach to learning.

- Infuse the hard work and seriousness with humor, appreciation, and celebration.
- *Ask for* 10 to 25 percent more effort and *get* 10 to 25 percent more effort.
- Create an environment that supports and engenders extreme clarity, extreme participation, and extreme practice.

Extreme Clarity, Participation, and Practice

From your initial contact with a learner, to the way you set up your room, to how you present your content, generate meaning, assess learning, and apply it, whether you are in a classroom, boardroom, or a virtual classroom, ENGAGE mindfully considers it all. This model is heavy on learning through hands-on exercises, novelty, creative challenges, hard work, fun, assessment, connection, and celebration of new learning. It revolutionizes typical teaching methods and rebalances the learning equation by replacing the passive, teacher-centric approach with an active, learner-centered approach that emphasizes extreme clarity, extreme participation, and extreme practice. These secret ingredients (I guess they aren't secret anymore), along with generous praise, positive intent, gratitude, and support multiply learner success. ENGAGE is a comprehensive way to design instruction that is the core of an overall learning system that drives outcomes and mobilizes revitalized resources—intellect, talent, ability—what I call brilliance.

Connect—Inspire—ENGAGE

At the heart of the design is a continuous dynamic flow of activity: Connect—Inspire—ENGAGE (see Figure 3.2). This trio of elements catalyzes the brilliance teachers and learners possess, the power of the new content, and the ENGAGE Learning Design. The design continuously draws on it and results in a synergy that energizes the brilliance zone.

Figure 3.2. Dynamic Flow

This dynamic flow of connecting, inspiring, and engaging will be a constant presence as you go through the six steps of the ENGAGE process. Its energy will be like a heart pumping the life force through the ENGAGE experience. The teacher inspires curiosity and learning at deeper and deeper levels and provides the tools and strategies for intense participation and practice. The learner engages with the new content to grasp it in multiple ways and to understand the content so that it is meaningful, applicable, and transformative. Throughout this cycle, there is a constant pattern of connection through feedback. It essentially becomes a self-energizing, regenerative process. You will recognize this flow in the six steps and learn to incorporate it into your own design and best practices.

Six Steps to ENGAGE

Let's take a brief look at the ENGAGE Model by way of introduction to these steps so that you have an idea of what's coming up. You might even be able to use some of it if you have a meeting in an hour. Each of the six steps in the model will be clarified and articulated in Chapters 4 through 10. You will then receive the full experience and be as "engaged" as possible as you discover the specific tools, strategies, and practices for implementing each step in this powerful instructional design. (Note that Chapter 10 focuses on how to ENGAGE in the virtual classroom.) Along the way, insights, stories, and concrete examples will help you connect your content to each step and develop your own application of the many strategies.

Step 1: Energize Learners.   Effective learning that drives outcomes, creates results, and transfers to action happens over time. If you're going to unleash people's brilliance, you need to give them a chance to pull forward preexisting information—what they already know. You also need to challenge their thought patterns and stimulate their curiosity about what you are teaching. To do this, you want to energize and focus your learners early and throughout the session. In this step, you will learn how to do that through many practices, such as sending information prior to the learning event to get them excited and curious about your topic; meeting and greeting people and learning something about them; setting up your room to stimulate curiosity, enhance active learning, and make learning fun; getting people physically moving; involving people actively with your content as soon as possible; reminding learners of their value, and appreciating them and their hard work; challenging them with questions and listening to them; and sharing your promise for the day.

Step 2: Navigate Content.   In this step, you present your compelling content. This is where you make your greatest investment of time, energy, and talent, because this is when the neural connections are made that are necessary for the kind of learning and change in behavior you want to take place. You will learn to present content in small chunks—digestible pieces; involve learners in varied, interactive experiences to understand concepts; create valuable tools for repeated use during learning practice and assessment; check in with learners and provide feedback; and assess and value their learning along the way. Navigating new content is the heart of the ENGAGE Model.

Step 3: Generate Meaning.   In this step of the process, guided by the teacher, learners determine the significance of this new content in their lives. They ascribe its meaning, purpose, relevance, and value. Using the art of inquiry, you help your learners arrive at what is genuinely meaningful and relevant to them. This relevancy inspires commitment to learning and moves the intentions and aspirations into action.

Step 4: Apply to Real World.   This is the step where you help learners apply—actually put into practice in their world—what they've learned. In this step, the transition from "knowing" to "doing" takes place as learners struggle to make sense of the new learning in context. Learners leave this phase ready to transfer action to practice and incorporate the learning in their lives. This step energizes both you and your learners. You will learn all about their world, see the application of your content through their eyes, and continue to improve your content as well as your teaching by weaving in the collective wisdom of the group.

Step 5: Gauge and Celebrate.   During this step of the learning design, whether it is a one-hour, full-day, or three-day session, you show people how much they have learned and assess it. As you involve the learners in the assessment activity, you also generate enthusiasm, appreciation, and a sense of wonder around all they have learned. This assessment time is a big celebration. A key principle of this phase is helping people realize the power that comes with this new knowledge because they have expanded choices.

Step 6: Extend Learning to Action.   How often have you learned something new, and despite your best intentions to apply it right away in your life, you just didn't do it? Sometimes it takes a reminder or motivation from another source. We'll explore this in Chapter 9, with an action plan, buddy system, and other practices you will implement so that your learners will continue getting results after applying their learning in real-life situations.

Ready to ENGAGE?

Figure 3.3 synthesizes this chapter, containing all the concepts and best practices in the ENGAGE Model. As you can see, it is packed with activities. You can use this tool as a reference to help deepen your own understanding of the instructional design as a whole, and to see how each step builds on the others. It will give you a view of where you are heading, and you can use it to create a quick learning design tool using your own content. At the end of each chapter, you will find a more thorough template that you can fill in with the strategies you would like to use. By the time we finish all six steps, you will have abundant strategies and resources for building your own one-page synthesis or job aid and making your content come alive with the ENGAGE Model.

It's time for the full ENGAGE experience. As you work through Chapters 4 through 10, you will see a multitude of best practices and strategies

ENGAGE Model to Design the Learner Experience

From your content, with an understanding of learners, you will: (choose some from each)

E—Energize Learners	*Before Session:* Focus and excite	❏ E-mail invitation ❏ Impact map ❏ Letter ❏ Book, article, study guide ❏ Pre-assessment ❏ Podcast
	Room:	❏ Protein snacks ❏ Posters/Visuals ❏ Music
	To Start Session: Thank and involve immediately	❏ Greet individually _____ ❏ Opening question _____ ❏ Interactive activity _____ ❏ Key outcomes/Goals for the day _____
N—Navigate Content	*Teach:*	❏ Lecture, demonstrate ❏ Stories ❏ Experience, then label ❏ Handouts ❏ Video/DVD ❏ Auditory ❏ Visual ❏ Kinesthetic
	Review:	❏ Card sort ❏ Role-play ❏ Journaling ❏ Case studies ❏ Game ❏ Song ❏ Mind map ❏ Mini-Peer Teach ❏ Team activity
G—Generate Meaning	Move to long-term memory	❏ Ask: What is the value of using this new content/mode? ❏ Flip chart: What would the benefits of using this content be to you/others/your organization? ❏ What does this new learning mean for you? ❏ How will this learning help you? ❏ What did you learn? ❏ What does it mean?
A—Apply to Real World	Demonstrate skills	❏ Skills to apply _____ ❏ Learning lab ❏ Highly paid experts ❏ Cross training ❏ Real-world practice ❏ Team analysis ❏ Design own model ❏ Action learning
G—Gauge and Celebrate	Look how much you learned!	❏ Crossword puzzle ❏ Five visible signs ❏ Group mind map ❏ Create an acronym ❏ *Jeopardy* or other quiz show ❏ Stump the panel ❏ Quiz (multiple choice, fill in, true/false) ❏ Create a presentation to teach others ❏ End with story: Create an emotional commitment
E—Extend Learning to Action	Act on intentions	Recognize and reward: ❏ E-mail tips ❏ Gather and share success stories ❏ Podcast ❏ Contest/award for who used it most ❏ e-Newsletter ❏ 1:1 coaching to support learning ❏ Lunch and Learn ❏ Business impact/dollarize contest ❏ Create a support network ❏ Send out follow-up summary

Figure 3.3. The ENGAGE Synthesis/Job Aid

for each step of the ENGAGE Model to help you create an engaging design and implement the Brilliance Learning System. You will see and experience, through your imagination and selected exercises, how they work together to connect, inspire, and ENGAGE learners in an optimal learning experience.

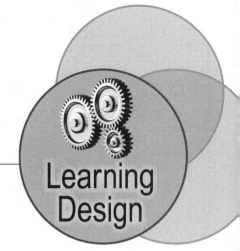
Learning Design

CHAPTER 4

Step 1: Energize Learners

E	• **Energize Learners**
N	• Navigate Content
G	• Generate Meaning
A	• Apply to Real World
G	• Gauge and Celebrate
E	• Extend Learning to Action

L earning begins with powerful first impressions. One of the keys to successfully engaging people during a learning session is to ignite their passion and commitment about the topic *ahead of time.* How you connect with participants and engage them *before* they show up for the learning session, as well as during the session before you launch into your new content, will drive their overall motivation to learn. Your goal is to have them arrive with smiles on their faces, eager, thinking about the subject, and ready to enhance their preexisting knowledge.

This chapter is all about the prelaunch before getting into your topic or core content as well as what to do to focus and energize people to start the session. It has multiple parts that cover everything from materials sent to learners before the learning event to techniques for ensuring you make a positive first impression and capture attention once learners arrive. Most importantly, this section offers a variety of strategies for "priming the pump," all of which are meant to pique the participant's curiosity about the topic, awaken any preexisting knowledge they have on the subject, and enable you to focus their attention on the value of your new knowledge. Ultimately, you will link their curiosity and knowledge to build their competence and commitment—a powerful connection to drive learning into action and unlock brilliance. Research has shown that the degree to which people are committed to utilizing information directly correlates to the strength of their practice, as well as the degree to which change actually occurs.[1]

Presession: Stimulate Engagement before Participants Show Up

Entice Learners and Highlight Genuine Benefits

Today's learners are pulled in many directions and have access to a multitude of options vying for their time and attention. How do you stand out from the rest and capture—or should I say recapture?—their attention when they first hear from you about your class or meeting? A great way to explore possibilities in answer to that question is for you to step into your learners' shoes and consider *What has energized and engaged them in learning before an actual event?*

REFLECTION: Exercise

MOTIVATED TO LEARN

Think about what it has taken for you to give up work, family, or private time to learn something new.

- What do you remember about a particular class you attended that motivated you to feel excited before you even got there?

- What was it about the sign-up materials (physical ones such as a brochure or flyer, or virtual ones such as an e-mail or electronic invitation)—the title, headings, bulleted benefits, description, or images—that reeled you in?

- What did the teacher do to make your specific presence (again, physical or virtual) at her class seem special?

Do Your Homework

A quick Internet search of classes on your subject could reveal a lot about how others are going about capturing the attention of your learners. Learning from collective wisdom often frees our own clarity of purpose.

Focus on factors that can make you stand out. Typically, the materials state very clearly what the class is about and what the benefits are to the attendee.

Use Visual and Written Testimonials

People love images of other people who are really enjoying themselves, and testimonials from previous participants who have taken the class are often the best endorsements. Sometimes a picture says it all, especially when the picture says something like, "Wow! This class rocked my world!" Strong endorsements and unequivocal enthusiasm are great invitations. Realize that you are not just asking people to a meeting or a workshop, you are also asking them to give up some of their valuable time. You want to make sure that everything you do says, "This class is for *you*. I value you, and I'm going to take good care of you in this session. You are going to learn something fabulous that's going to help you solve a problem, overcome a challenge, or do what you want to do in your life."

Personalize the Invitation

Imagine this: you walk into your office and discover on your desk an envelope with a small candy bar taped to it. You open it and find a handwritten note from your manager inviting you to the upcoming Situational Self Leadership seminar. She expresses her gratitude to you for all you do, and she invites you to come share and learn in the upcoming session. She closes the note with an insight about you. Two days later, you receive an e-mail giving you the login and password for the mini e-learning introduction to the upcoming class, with a request to listen within the next two days. Later that day, while listening to the 15-minute kickoff webinar, you are asked to read all the objectives for the upcoming class and make a list of projects and objectives you are currently working on where you think this course might help you be even more successful. You are asked to run that list by your manager within the next 48 hours. What do you think? Is there more benefit to you when you walk into a seminar after you have had all this pre-event engagement? What a difference!

In addition to an e-learning introduction and webinar with accompanying meaningful activities, there are other options for pre-learning event engagement. Just be careful not to go overboard. Send either a book or an article, not both, and only send something of real value. Figure 4.1 provides a variety of options for you to consider.

Energizing Pre-Learning Event Activities	
Books 	Before a session, you can send participants a book to level the playing field and do what in brain science is known as "reticular activation." A book helps learners think about what they already know about the subject. This way, they have already done a lot of pre-thinking before they arrive in class, which is helpful in connecting them to the new content they will learn.
Articles	Send an article, no more than five pages, that you or another authority has written on the subject. Alternatively, you can send an article that relates to your topic and is valuable. This offers learners the opportunity to do some thinking about the topic before they show up.

Figure 4.1.   Additional Pre-Learning Event Activities

Energizing Pre-Learning Event Activities	
Study guides	Depending on what you send, you may want to include a very clear study guide. This is a workbook that goes with the article or book you send. It strategically focuses on key components of the material you want learners to pay attention to. By answering questions, learners come ready to learn and deepen their understanding about the content you're about to present.
Questions to think about **Best Boss** Behaviors | Feelings	It may be helpful to provide a list of questions for participants to think about in regard to your topic. For example, if you're going to teach about leadership, you might have them think about the best leader they know. Or if you are teaching listening skills, have them answer questions about the best listeners they know: What do they actually do? What enables them to listen? What's the impact of great listening?
Interview questions **Interview protocol** Interview two people before your Legendary Service class. **1.** What is our greatest strength in serving customers? **2.** What keeps us from providing Legendary Service to our customers? **3.** If you were CEO, what would you do first?	Another idea for pre-work is to send your participants a set of interview questions. They can use these questions to interview other people to learn what they think about the topic. Your job is to come up with the questions *you* had when you began to research your topic.
Podcast welcome	Participants receive a link with a welcome from you, or an author of the material, or a senior leader in the organization.

Figure 4.1. (Continued)

61

Energizing Pre-Learning Event Activities	
Agenda in picture form	An agenda gives the mind a snapshot of the journey. Like taking a trip in a car, the brain mentally checks off milestones, gaining energy and motivation until arriving at the destination.
Impact map	Rob Brinkerhoff[2] and Dennis Dressler designed a system of improving the transfer of learning to doing that has participants complete an impact map before they learn. On the map, they determine their organizational, team, and individual goals, and link objectives from the course to goal achievement. This clear line of sight from course objective to goals increases learning transfer from about 20 percent to about 80 percent.[3]
Testimonials from previous participants	Sharing testimonials from previous participants in the pre-work materials increases initial commitment and receptivity to learning.
Video/DVD welcome	A video or DVD welcome that inspires participants, shares outcomes, and invites them to do some pre-thinking shows a genuine commitment from senior leaders to the outcome of the learning initiative. Subject matter experts might also be invited to create a short video, having people think about what the upcoming topic might mean to their world.
Questions to previous graduates	Including a few interview questions that participants can ask previous program graduates will enable them to find pertinent information, get excited about the upcoming class, and have their brain ready for the new learning.

Figure 4.1.   (Continued)

E	• Energize Learners
N	• Navigate Content
G	• Generate Meaning
A	• Apply to Real World
G	• Gauge and Celebrate
E	• Extend Learning to Action

Energizing Pre-Learning Event Activities	
Panel of graduates to give testimonials	Occasionally, it is fun to have a couple of previous graduates come to the class, either when kicking it off or before lunch, to share key learnings they have had and to fire up the participants about what's to come during your session.
Relevant quotations to inspire	Keeping a file of quotations relevant to your subject and printing them out on paper with cool pictures adds color and interest, and deepens learning and inspiration to your subject matter.
Icebreaker goal activity	If you're teaching business content, a great icebreaker activity would be to begin the session by having people talk about their current goals. Have them make a list of goals they or their team are currently working on. Throughout your session as you're teaching different concepts, ask participants to relate how this content might help them achieve their goals.
Pictures of past graduates on wall with quotes	Put pictures of past graduates on the wall with quotes or testimonials from them. This is an inviting way to build community and share the successes of your program.
Ask, "What do you want to be/feel/do as a result of this program?"	This is an activity you might conduct after you've shared the objectives of your class. Have learners go to flip charts and create three columns: *What do you want to (1) BE, (2) FEEL, and (3) DO as a result of this program?* After five minutes, have people report out. The goal is to create a target in their own minds of how the learning will apply in their day-to-day life.

Figure 4.1. (Continued)

Environment: Set the Stage

In addition to readying the learners before they show up, you need to prepare the location where you are going to teach. (This applies in physical interactions as well as virtual ones. In virtual training, which is covered in depth in Chapter 10, you would prepare your virtual environment via technology using the same principles.) It's a bit like getting ready for a party: you need to anticipate your guests' needs, do everything you can to make them feel comfortable and welcome, and make the experience novel and fun. You want to stimulate learning and creativity while making them feel relaxed and at the center of this particular universe.

Pique Curiosity Early

When you bring people together for a meeting or workshop, you want them to feel as if they are walking into a posh hotel or spa, but you also want them to be energized. Think of a Ritz-Carlton with theme park surprises!

The physical surroundings communicate an important message to guests. They say that the people behind the scenes care and want us to feel important—being there means that we will get our needs met. In learning, getting one's needs met means stimulating and energizing neural pathways and connections. The brain likes novelty.

Setting up your room can be as easy as putting a few posters or written quotes on the wall, playing music, and laying out healthy snacks in colorful bowls or trays. Consider some other simple surprises that boost learning. Remember to think the way you would if you were having a party—you *are* entertaining in a profound way.

- As part of your pre-event connection, you can ask participants to bring a favorite quote with them, and they can put them up on the walls. One of my favorite interactive learning tools is Magnetic Poetry Big Words—you can incorporate the use of the magnetic words with flip charts and computers to write vision statements or stories, or for many other purposes.

- Instead of using commonplace bowls and trays, serve healthy snacks in less conventional containers, maybe with a theme.

- Decorate tables with flowers, stacks of books or magazines, masks, transparent jars filled with colored balls.

- Lay sheets of paper across the tables, and fill a couple of cups or glasses with pencils, crayons, or markers so everyone can use them

E	• Energize Learners
N	• Navigate Content
G	• Generate Meaning
A	• Apply to Real World
G	• Gauge and Celebrate
E	• Extend Learning to Action

to draw, doodle, or write. (You can design an activity that intentionally incorporates these.)

- Place fascinating manipulative toys or other objects on the table for the kinesthetic learners to play with. Smart puzzle toys that you have to figure out how to put together or take apart can be extremely engaging, challenging, and fun.

- Blocks in a wide variety of textures, shapes, colors, and sizes invite collaboration: try some with magnetic connectors, or others that require builders to attach them by squishing them together, such as LEGO bricks.

Think of your room and its physical décor as a set with props. Change things often. Rearrange some of the seating, put up different posters on the

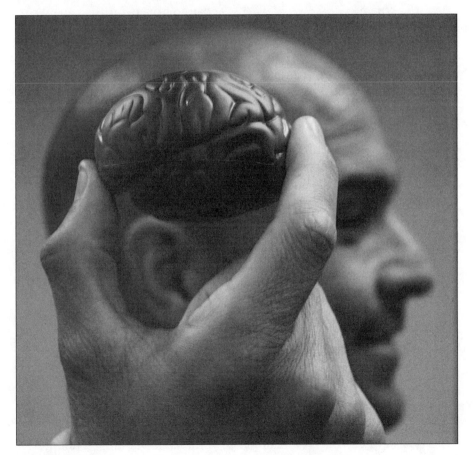

Toys stimulate the brain and keep kinesthetic learners engaged.

walls, hang or project examples of high-quality thinking, or move objects around. You could exchange manipulative toys and objects between tables, or put out something new in one area after each break. See if people notice and start drifting that way to see what is coming next. Making sure there is a lot of novelty and variety doesn't mean you have to rearrange everything—even small changes matter. For instance, chairs can be moved and turned. Even a desk or conference room can hold something that is an interesting focal point, useful for shifting thinking. By changing something occasionally, you spark attention and engage people to think in new ways.

Many years ago, when I was an assistant principal, I worked with a sixth grade teacher named Erica who was known for her "Surprise Mondays." Every Monday she prepared a big table on the side of the room with an assortment of objects that she covered with a big sheet. With a simple table and sheet, she attached an atmosphere of mystery to the whole enterprise. The students couldn't wait for Monday to arrive, for the time when Erica would remove the sheet. They loved seeing what was hidden underneath, and finding out how it related to what they were learning. The anticipation in the room was palpable as the students gathered around the table. Eyes would widen, and they would all lean in. One week there were shells for her oceanography lessons, another week there were toy cars for physics and motion, and still another week there was a book, such as *The Diary of Anne Frank* or a classic on the theme of science fiction or the supernatural. Whatever Erica had hidden under the sheet each Monday was used throughout that week in writing exercises, math, science, social studies, and art. She used the brain's love of novelty and desire to make connections to energize and focus learners. By the weekend, all of her students—and even students who weren't in her class—were curious and wondering what next Monday's surprise was going to be.

During the Session: Energize Learners upon Arrival

Make a Great First Impression

Tony Robbins always has great music that precedes him at his events. Last time I heard him speak, U2's "Beautiful Day" was blasting, inspiring all of us to jump up and sing along. Music always makes me feel as if something exciting is going to happen. It is so uplifting and energizing to have music versus a typical PowerPoint presentation with someone fiddling around in the

E	• Energize Learners
N	• Navigate Content
G	• Generate Meaning
A	• Apply to Real World
G	• Gauge and Celebrate
E	• Extend Learning to Action

front of the room. Tony follows the great music with a big welcome, poses a big question, and asks you to stand up (shifts your state) and share your answer with the person next to you. The music, movement, and immediate involvement all create energy, whether he is talking to 30 people or 10,000. Those cues to the brain say, "Pay attention. This interaction is important."

Energizing people means getting them to be active participants versus passive listeners as soon as you possibly can. You want to begin by creating the energy needed throughout the session for learners to do the difficult work of developing a new competence. Teaching and learning are highly personal. The initial relationship you develop with your learners either accelerates or inhibits the learning. The faster you create a connection with your participants, the faster their brains open up and become receptive to the fabulous content you are teaching. And the faster you get participants comfortable with each other—realizing that the other participants in the room are people just like them, trying to do their best—the faster people will open up to share new ideas, fears, and challenges about the learning, and participate at their highest level.

I greet every participant I can (depending on the size of my audience) as they walk in and ask them a bit about their world. I want to know each of them and make a personal connection while expressing appreciation for their being there. I also introduce them to each other and get them to sit together if it is a large room. Showing you care enough to say "Hi" and having them introduce themselves shifts their energy and helps them become present while feeling connected.

This personal welcome, along with the pre-learning event activities, is to let the learners know that this is going to be a wonderful experience, that you value them, their time, and their commitment, and that *you* are a person they are going to love learning with.

How do you convey to all participants that they are important? Everyone has to develop his own way of doing this so that it is comfortable for him. Whether it is a keynote speech, classroom training, or meeting I am facilitating, I want to convey that everyone is important. One way I achieve this goal is by asking questions early, being an authentic listener, and tucking away what I've learned during our brief conversations so I can use it later in a meaningful way.

Get People Talking

Once everyone has gathered, most facilitators "talk at" participants for 10 to 15 minutes or longer before they let anyone else talk. I like to switch things up. I think that the faster you get your learners talking about relevant, interesting topics, the faster you excite them, activate their interest and commitment to your content, and confirm that they are important.

When it is time to sit down, I always tell people to sit wherever they are most comfortable, and to make sure they are sitting with other people so they can share information and build community.

In my Master of Science coursework in executive leadership and M.B.A. classes on individual and organizational learning, I begin by teaching the concept of *maximizing learning*. I kick things off with an activity designed to set up all the concepts that will follow. It is an easy, low-risk activity I borrowed from Susan Rundle, President of Performance Concepts International and specialist in learning application and productivity.[4] It is best to begin with low-risk activities and gradually move to higher-risk activities to build trust, just as you want to move from simple to more complex concepts.

Here's how the activity works:

1. Students think about their best learning experience. They picture what made it a great learning experience. Then, on four sticky notes, they write the elements or strategies they need to really learn something that sticks.

2. After they finish writing, they post all the sticky notes on a board at the front of the room. I randomly select three notes from the board and hand a group of three notes to each student.

3. Next, the students circulate and gather, exchange, steal, or take notes left on the board until they each end up with three sticky notes that really fit their experience. This is where the fun comes in. This activity breaks down walls and builds connectedness in a very low-risk way. People are pretty creative about how they capture the sticky notes that sing to their individual needs. There is a lot of laughter and liveliness as they find the best ideas for how they want to learn.

4. After each person has their three sticky notes, they get into a group of individuals who have *similar* learning needs. They collaborate on making a poster, with pictures only, that depicts what they need to be able to learn.

5. The group then does a "field trip" from poster to poster, with the individuals who created the poster asking people what they think the pictures mean.

E	• Energize Learners
N	• Navigate Content
G	• Generate Meaning
A	• Apply to Real World
G	• Gauge and Celebrate
E	• Extend Learning to Action

By the end of this activity, everyone has talked with just about everyone else in the class, shared what they needed in order to maximize their learning, and had a lot of fun in an activity where they were discussing, drawing, guessing, and physically moving around the room. Meanwhile, they've also bonded over the key concepts I will ultimately teach, and they have worked pretty hard.

When they share key learnings from the activity, participants often notice that no one said that they learn best by having someone talking at them while using PowerPoint. Not one group has ever said that. This introductory activity positions them to *discover* this very important learning. They realize that the typical modes of teaching are not necessarily effective, and this realization hooks them into the concept of the day: to maximize learning, they need to embrace new concepts, think in new ways, and teach so they facilitate learning rather than stifle it. The first activity of the session *involves all the learners in the process of discovery of the principles I want to teach throughout the course, and they use those principles (interactivity, speaking, etc.) to reach the learning.* Aha!

Ask Challenging Questions

Another great way to create active participation early is to start off with a provocative question (see Figure 4.2). Depending on my topic and audience, I might ask a question such as "Who was your best coach?" "Who was your best boss or leader?" "What was the best team you have ever been on?" or "What was your best performance review?" Follow your question by having participants write their answers on flip chart pages, and keep them handy for later. When it comes time for you to teach the actual content, participants can interact with their own material. They can label their responses based on the models you've been teaching, and realize that they can draw

If you're talking about:	The energized, focused question could be:
Coaching	Who was your best coach?
Leadership	Who was your best boss/leader?
Teamwork	What was the best team you've ever been on?
Performance reviews	What was your best performance review?

Figure 4.2. Provocative Questions

from their preexisting knowledge of this topic to connect to the new knowledge. This connection lengthens the time of retention and makes it more meaningful.

Rally Mutual Commitment

Helping each learner realize that he or she has something unique and valuable to contribute is important. Whatever the activity you choose, connecting learners through shared experiences builds relationships and creates a community of learners with a mutual commitment. Even a simple exercise in which learners get to know each other by talking about their interests can elicit bonding and reveal a profound mutual connection.

You can facilitate this important connection with a flip chart activity, a table discussion activity, a puzzle, or in a multitude of other ways. I often have people get into pairs and assign them the job of introducing each other to the group. This builds an early bond, and is a bit more fun than just introducing yourself. I often ask them to share one unique thing about someone in the group and the room decides which unique fact goes with which person. It creates a lively community when you learn someone used to work as the Chuck E. Cheese mouse, or someone else got kicked out of preschool. Quite fun! By having people start communicating with each other, they realize that *they* are the ones who are going to make or break their time together and that, fundamentally, we are all people trying to do our best. This bond strengthens the learning for everyone and lays the groundwork for supporting each other's success.

Call Out Gifts and Successes of Learners

While milling around to meet and talk with people prior to a customer service training session for managers, I met Bill, who manages a call center in Detroit, and Susan, who manages one in New Jersey. They were talking about how hard it is to do on-the-job training. It was great information for me to know that they shared this common concern. In the beginning of any session as well as throughout the session, I want learners to know that, although I have some great content to share with them, probably the most valuable knowledge and expertise to contribute comes from them and their world. I want to encourage them to offer it because everyone benefits. Much of the learning arises because of them. I rarely say this, because at various points in my talk I get to illustrate it. For example, in the customer service training when the challenge arises of how to train

E	• Energize Learners
N	• Navigate Content
G	• Generate Meaning
A	• Apply to Real World
G	• Gauge and Celebrate
E	• Extend Learning to Action

people while they are doing their job, I might say, "Bill, who manages a call center in Detroit, and Susan from New Jersey know this is a great challenge." And then I might say to the rest of the learners, "How have you overcome this challenge? How have you trained people? How have you gotten people off the phones long enough to train them in this new strategy we are implementing?" Then we listen to what they have to say and engage others in the conversation. I have now shown them that I value their experience and the great contributions they bring to this class. You are going to give your learners your unique model and content, but the only way it comes to life is through the efforts, commitment, and current reality of the participants, so a big part of your job is engendering that.

You can use this same strategy in teleconferencing or in any virtual learning session where you can talk with participants ahead of time or during breaks. Then you can incorporate what you learned from them to engage and value them in the process of learning. You always want to build commonalities and a strong sense of community.

In *The Talent Code,*[5] Daniel Coyle references a study showing that initial commitment to learning drives outcome and utilization of learning over time. Those with high commitment initially have three times the learning of those who say, "I'm not sure I'm going to use this." So your job as facilitator is to make sure that you really value participants and facilitate their commitment to learning by demonstrating the benefits early on.

Value and Unite Participants

Early in the session, take the time to unite the group with their common strengths by calling out the gift that they are to the world. This is another way of valuing them, and you can't do too much of that. When I facilitated training at Dade Behring (now Siemens), all the participants were medical techs—the people behind the scenes who draw, test, and analyze blood and do other vital jobs that are rarely appreciated. I started the day off with the question "Who is the backbone of the medical industry?" They yelled out, "We are!" Then I said, "Who do all the doctors depend on for accurate information and data?" and they yelled, "Us!" I wanted every person to hear, "I know your world, and I know people in general don't realize your value." Why do you do this? Why do you start off with something that makes everyone in the room feel that you know them? You do this to validate them and their very existence. Declare that they make a difference in the world, that the world would not be the same without them. Validating the uniqueness of each participant strengthens their own sense of personal significance and unites them all in their common value. This also demonstrates the respect you have for all that they are—their years of experience and their deep knowledge.

Express Gratitude

Thank people generously and often. Thanking people for showing up lets them know that you understand their world, and it opens them up for what is to come. Acknowledge that you know their lives are busy, sometimes even overwhelming, so you know what a big deal it is that they took the time from their families, friends, work, or from their own slice of private time to be at this learning event. Express gratitude in the beginning and through-out the session. The power of appreciation is highly underused. Notice the positive things you see going on, even the small things, and acknowledge them. Gratitude energizes people, makes them feel valued (as they should be), and makes them want to give more of themselves. In writing about "appreciating authentically," Kevin Cashman says, "Multiply your leadership energy through the practice of genuine appreciation."[6]

Share Your Promise

During this early portion of the session, be sure to state clearly the specific outcomes or results. You are asking people to make a commitment to learning for that session. You are asking for their time, energy, attention, and hard work. What is your promise to them? You might start off by saying, "Today we're going to learn about leadership (or coaching, or being a high-performance team, etc.). My promise to you is that, at the end of this session, you will walk out the door knowing how to be that best leader (or best coach, high-performance team, etc.)." Or you might say, "You will learn three skills: _____, _____, and _____." This is where all your preparation in creating clear outcomes in Chapter 2 comes into play. Your job—no, not just your job, but your privilege—at this time is to share your vision of the learning outcomes clearly and succinctly while helping people visualize the big picture—what they will be able to do differently because they were present for that hour, day, or week. This vision is the story that you and the learners will breathe into existence by working together.

At some point, maybe even at several points, each of your learners may have asked himself or herself, "What's in it for me to learn to do this? Why am I here?" These are intelligent questions. Even though you spelled it out in your descriptive sign-up materials, you need to drive it home again after they hear the specific outcomes. Remind participants why they have made an intelligent choice; what pain is this learning going to ease; and that this is a valuable use of their precious time and energy.

Listen Early and Often

When I stop to think about directing my content and my teaching to my learners, I usually ask myself three questions. I call it the W-cubed Model: *What* am I (the teacher or speaker) going to share (my content)? *Why* is it important to them (their outcomes)? *What* is the current experience of the participants in relation to that content and how will it be improved (learning design)? It's my job to answer those questions clearly as I plan my content and facilitate the learning. If I listen carefully, I'll get much of what I need from the participants to connect what is important to them to what they are learning and how it will improve their lives. However, like appreciation, listening is another underused power tool.

When I teach leadership, I often start off with one of those provocative questions I mentioned earlier, such as "What are your leadership challenges?" Then I really *listen* to what their challenges are. The mistake many teachers, speakers, trainers, and managers make is that they think asking the question is merely a bridge for them to take off into their prepared, carved-in-stone message. They go through the motions of engaging people in responses, but they do not *listen or actually hear them*. This is a big mistake because you lose a teachable moment. Such questions are meaningless when they are asked rhetorically. After you ask a big question like that, you definitely want to *really listen* to what people have to say and, if possible, weave it into your future comments and concepts you are sharing.

Regardless of what you've prepared and where you're going next in your outline, you want to thank learners for their insights. Acknowledge the substance of their challenge and the emotions involved, as well as the impact on their lives. By doing so, you facilitate greater transfer of new content to action because people have released the emotion attached to their pain. If someone says, "I just lost two out of seven people, and we are still having to do the same workload," a facilitator could say, "Oh, that's awful," and move on. Or the facilitator could think what might be involved in that and try to restate or articulate it back, saying, "Wow, it must have been unbelievably difficult to restructure everyone's roles and to keep people motivated to take on a pretty decent chunk of extra work in addition to all the current work they're doing." (See Figure 4.3.) Then the wise

> The mistake many teachers, speakers, trainers, and managers make is that they think asking the question is merely a bridge for them to take off into their prepared, carved-in-stone message.

73

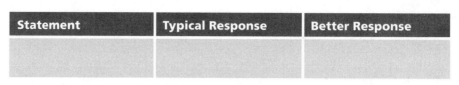

Statement	Typical Response	Better Response

Figure 4.3. Statement/Responses

facilitator takes it one step further and expresses gratitude to that participant for being there with all the additional work she must be doing, because you are going to help her do more in less time. You just linked this challenge to your content.

The underlying principle is to make sure you acknowledge the emotion around what the individual is saying; otherwise, the person doesn't feel heard. Someone who doesn't feel heard might even subliminally be a little irritated with you for asking a question and not acknowledging an answer. That builds a barrier to learning, and you want to make connections, not build walls. When you do an exercise like this, you want to make sure that you capture all the responses to your powerful questions in some way, because at the end of the session you want to go back to that person in the example and say, "How helpful is it for you to have learned the content we taught today?" Using the leadership example, you might link back to this person and say, "How will the concepts you have learned today help you do more with less?"

Spotlight Key Themes

How do you share what it is you're going to talk about? You could have three PowerPoints that have the three main concepts, or you could have posters on the wall with your key points, or maybe something on the cover of your workbook that continually reminds people and subconsciously helps them get to the core of what it's all about—the reason they are there.

> I've always felt that it was my job as a teacher, principal, speaker, and leader to connect people to what is important to them.

Link Learning to What Really Matters

It is pivotal to your success moving forward to have people realize the importance of what they are going to be learning. They have to arrive at the realization of its importance and value it for themselves; you can't tell them what it is.

I've always felt that it was my job as a teacher, principal, speaker, and leader to connect people to what is important to them. By helping them identify what is important or just reminding them what really matters to them, I can help them connect to their passion and pur-

E	• Energize Learners
N	• Navigate Content
G	• Generate Meaning
A	• Apply to Real World
G	• Gauge and Celebrate
E	• Extend Learning to Action

pose, and demonstrate the relevance of this new content I am teaching. This connection is a powerful agent in driving learning to application. One way to link "what matters" to the learning of new content is to provide a section in a workbook or on a separate worksheet called "What Really Matters" or "Learning Objectives." Your learners go down this list of content issues and place a check next to the things that are really important to them. You do this so people instantly have buy-in. They're saying, "I want to focus on *this*. I've put a checkmark here. I choose this as important to me." That's instant commitment or buy-in right away to what you're going to teach, and acknowledgment that it is going to be of value to them.

Another way to accomplish this personally chosen commitment is to elicit what is important directly from them through an activity such as the K/W/L chart (Figure 4.4), in which they express what's important, what made them show up, and what they really hope to get out of the session. Pull from them what really matters so you can connect your information with their needs.

Topic	K **What You Know**	W **What You Want to Know**	L **What You've Learned**
Listening	• It's difficult. • Not many do it well. • It takes time. • It involves body language.	• What can help me become a better listener? • Is there a model for listening that will trigger me as I try to listen? • Will I be able to practice today so I really get the skills? • It involves eye contact.	• To be completed at end of session

Figure 4.4. K/W/L Chart

K/W/L Charts Activate Knowledge. In this activity, participants write three columns on a flip chart with the headings K, W, and L. The K stands for what they already *know* about this topic, W is for what they *want* to know, and L—to be filled out at the end—is what they have actually *learned*.

This activity is an effective way to fulfill my goal for this first part of the session, which is *to help participants realize what they already know about the topic, link it to what the new content offers,* and *connect that to what their hopes are.* It gets them actively involved right at the beginning so they feel that it's about them and their experience, and it demonstrates that there's a pivotal need for what they are about to learn. In addition, it helps you fulfill another goal: at the end of the day or at the end of the hour, you can use the "What You've Learned" portion to move the learning into action.

Learners are now ready to get the core of the new learning. They are focused, energized, and receptive to learning. You have triggered the part of the brain that says, "Hmmm . . . important information coming—pay attention!"

REFLECTION: Exercise

ENERGIZE AND FOCUS LEARNERS

- What has been the most energizing, memorable strategy someone has used with you in a learning situation?

- What two key learnings from this chapter will you put into your session as you teach?

E	• Energize Learners
N	• Navigate Content
G	• Generate Meaning
A	• Apply to Real World
G	• Gauge and Celebrate
E	• Extend Learning to Action

Energize Learners
DO-IT-YOURSELF TEMPLATE

PRE-SESSION

_____
_____
_____
_____
_____
_____
_____
_____
_____
_____
_____
_____
_____
_____
_____
_____
_____
_____

❏ Personal invitation
❏ Welcome letter
❏ E-mail invite
❏ Pre-interview questions
❏ Senior leader endorsement
❏ Journey map/learner map/agenda in pictures
❏ Timeline
❏ Preassessment
❏ Book or article
❏ Study guides
❏ Questions to think about
❏ Podcast
❏ Prerecorded webinar
❏ Impact map
❏ Testimonials from previous participants
❏ Video/DVD
❏ Inspirational quotes
" _____ "

STARTING THE SESSION

_____
_____
_____
_____
_____
_____
_____
_____
_____
_____
_____
_____
_____

❏ Energizing environment/novelty
  ❏ Toys for kinesthetic, pens, etc.
  ❏ Protein snacks, water
❏ Quotes, posters, visuals
❏ Music
❏ Greeting each participant and learning two facts
❏ Getting participants talking early
❏ Asking catchy opening question
" _____ "
❏ Initial activity/active participation
❏ Value statement to participants
" _____ "
❏ Key objectives/themes for the day
❏ My promise to you is: _____
❏ K/W/L chart

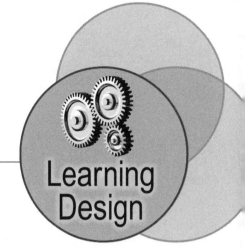

CHAPTER **5**

Step 2: Navigate Content

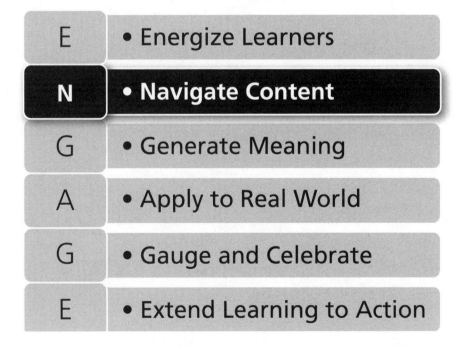

E	• Energize Learners
N	**• Navigate Content**
G	• Generate Meaning
A	• Apply to Real World
G	• Gauge and Celebrate
E	• Extend Learning to Action

When I was an assistant principal, we launched a life skills program. Every adult in the school worked with a small group of kids every morning for 15 to 20 minutes. In order to support the staff, I skimmed off all the most challenging kids so they wouldn't negatively impact anyone else's group interactions. I ended up with about 30 kids.

The only way I could get them to focus on their life skills lesson was to promise they could play a game show–style quiz the last half of the session. We divided the group into four teams, and each got a buzzer. I played Alex Trebek, the game show host, and in my revised *Jeopardy,* I asked a variety of questions from a range of fields. This gave everyone a chance to show their smarts: One kid may know a lot about combustion engines, another about geography, and another about the chemistry of making ice cream. One boy (let's call him Randy) was a small, skinny sixth grader with glasses and a mouth like an actor in an R-rated movie. His language and behavior often triggered the other kids to pick on him. Despite all my efforts to protect him, there was still a bit of teasing when he was late or wasn't paying attention. The kids—even these creative, divergent-thinking kids—in their own way had labeled him as semi-incompetent. Then, during one quiz, I asked, "What's the common name for aspirin?" and Randy's hand slammed the buzzer. He said, "Acetylsalicylic acid." In that same quiz I asked, "What does DNA stand for?" Randy's hand hit the buzzer again, and he answered, "Deoxyribonucleic acid." For a long moment, there was an awed silence in the room. Then his team cheered and clapped him on the back. His opportunity to be brilliant had arrived—he had "shown up"—and it reshaped his middle school career. In Randy's world, this was equivalent to making two hockey goals to win the game and trounce the opponent. With the utterance of his startling, brilliant answers, he earned the respect of every student present. The degrading comments ceased. Instead of treating him like a loser, the kids embraced him as *their* genius, their friend. He was one of them at last, and on *his* terms.

Think about what my role was in this transformational story. What did I do? I facilitated a quiz game, an active learning exercise, and asked questions on a variety of topics such as sports, history, and science so that everyone got to be smart and to help his or her team. I set the stage for brilliance to surface in a variety of ways and for building a shared community of learners.

E	• Energize Learners
N	**• Navigate Content**
G	• Generate Meaning
A	• Apply to Real World
G	• Gauge and Celebrate
E	• Extend Learning to Action

How to Navigate Your Content

How are you incorporating opportunities in your learning design for people to show up as geniuses in their own unique ways? This section is going to help you do just that—create brilliance, by design. "Navigate Content" is your time to present your content in varied, interactive ways.

But this chapter is not about *what* you are teaching. This chapter helps you make conscious choices about *how* you present and teach that content; how you "navigate" the content with your learners so that they develop a desired level of understanding of your new concepts. You'll do this by laying the groundwork with these principles and by using multiple strategies for learners to practice, such as:

- Set the stage for learners to interact with the content.
- Be clear.
- Offer activities for multiple learning styles so everyone gets to show up smart.
- Inspire learners to do hard work.
- Involve learners in a high level of activity that changes frequently.

How do people who feel brilliant show up? They show up very differently from people who think they are incompetent. Brilliant people have their hand in the air. They can't wait to blurt out the answer. They are not only on the edge of their seats, they are sometimes jumping out of them. They ask tough, insightful questions. They disclose when they don't get something because they really want to *get* this new information. You want to structure the design so people can bring the best of who they are to the learning experience. To make this mission possible, you need to create an environment and opportunities for *everyone*, not just the usual hand-wavers, to be present and alert and to unleash their best thoughts. How will you do this? You will simultaneously build the following framework into your activities/strategies for practice. This inner framework is how you teach learners your new concepts.

1. Focus learners on the target.
2. Help them *experience and label* the new information.
3. Drill down and *embed* on your key concepts *through interaction*.
4. Then *practice* the concepts and *check* for understanding.

Focus on the Target

How many times have you heard a teacher say something like, "I'm going to teach you three keys to leadership" (or high-quality service, or making smart investment choices). She has clarified her promise to you. She holds up her hand, looks you in the eye, and lists three commitments. There is a good reason that is a common practice, a best practice, for teachers. It's a declaration or a *challenge to the brain*. The brain is like a heat-seeking missile. If you say, "I'm going to teach you a model; I'm going to teach you to do three things," the brain thinks, "All right, I'm going to learn three things." Then your brain really works to learn those three things. Here's how it works.

Pretend you're going shopping for a black coat. You are basically a black coat heat-seeking missile. You're going to look everywhere (in physical stores or virtual ones online). You'll notice other things in your peripheral vision as you travel a path looking for that black coat, but you'll pass them by. You're on a mission: You want a black coat. You'll do the same thing if you want a pair of new jeans or a certain type of car. You'll disregard everything that's not that *one thing* you want, that target your brain is seeking. That same dynamic happens in learning. We can ignore all the distractions of our lives *if it's clear what we are going to learn*. So how do you teach your content? You start by stating the target—your objective—very clearly. Then you guide your learners through a dynamic flow, a cycle of learning that includes personal experience, realization that connects to that experience with the new content, presentation of the new content model, intense interaction with content, and then checking for understanding and practice.

Connect to Personal Experience, Then Label the Contents

Learners grasp the new learning in your content model better if you offer them the opportunity to *experience it first or link it to an experience that they have had*. That's right—immersing them in even a brief activity in which they experience a key aspect will link them to your concepts faster and more meaningfully. So think of a clever strategy, an interactive 15- to 20-minute activity where the goal is for them to experience one important concept that you are trying to teach.

At The Ken Blanchard Companies, one of the subjects I teach is Situational Leadership® II. This model teaches that people go through four stages of development as they move from a beginner to a self-reliant achiever on tasks or goals.[1] It doesn't matter whether you are learning to ski, to sell water purification systems, or to lead a corporate division. We all go through four stages of development, and each person is at a different stage depending on their goal or task. In our workshop, we teach participants that the faster they

E	• Energize Learners
N	• Navigate Content
G	• Generate Meaning
A	• Apply to Real World
G	• Gauge and Celebrate
E	• Extend Learning to Action

can identify their present level of development and that of each person on their staff, the faster their needs can be articulated and then met. Participants learn that there are four styles of leadership that match these four stages of development, and that most leaders only use one of the four styles.

When I teach this, I want awareness to come from the participants' own experience to accelerate the learning. I begin by talking about the four development levels and having participants think of a skill they are very proficient at now. Then I ask them to remember when they couldn't do it at all. This might be driving a stick shift car, skiing, using new computer software, playing a game, or solving a puzzle. I guide their memory to the beginning, when they first got the car or the skis or the software. I coax their recollection with some questions: "How did you feel? What was your competence? What was going on for you?" Then they write their first memory: "I was excited, but I didn't know what I was doing," "I had a friend talk me through the gears," or "I listened to tapes on the subject." I want them to recognize that, at first, they didn't have competence but were motivated, really fired up. They have described the first development level.

Next, I pull them through the second development level: "What happened when you tried driving the car, or tried skiing, or tried using the software?" They write about their second development level: "I kept falling down when I tried skiing," "I was discouraged because the car kept stalling when I popped the clutch too fast," or "The software wasn't as easy to use as I thought it would be." I pull them through the description of when they were still not competent and had lost some of their motivation or confidence. (But I don't *say* that yet, because they are not yet labeling it; they are just experiencing it.)

Then I talk to them about the third stage of development, where they were able to drive the car, ski, or use the software, but they were not fully confident. They describe themselves at that third stage of development, when they could do the task but were hesitant or a bit uncertain. I tell them to include as many details that show that they felt capable but just a little cautious.

Last, I have them describe the final stage of development, when they knew what they were doing and didn't really have to think about it. They felt highly competent and highly committed and could ski, drive, or use the software easily. When they have finished writing their experience, we go back and label it with the Situational Leadership® II terminology and the new model.

The goal is to have learners connect personally through their own experience to some aspect of what you are trying to teach. Then, you show them the actual model you want to teach through a lecture-style presentation, video, or interactive exercise. *They learn to label or identify the experience conceptually from their experience.* You drill down and elaborate on what it was that they just learned so they connect to the concepts. You then help them

> The goal is to have them personally experience some aspect of what you are trying to teach.

deepen their knowledge through more lecture or some kind of film, audiotape, video, or pictures where they feel the experience of the content you are trying to teach. By having the learning come from their experience, you are showing them that they already knew this but may not have had the language or context to make sense of it.

Create Statistical Face Validity

Let's say you are trying to focus your team on customer service. You start off by having people rate the general level of service they get in their lives from restaurants, banks, or call centers on a scale from 1 to 10. They raise their hand, or they come up and put an "X" on a flip chart. By rating their own experience with customer service and sharing it with a group, they realize that typically it's somewhere between a 3 and a 6 for the whole group. You can build on this by saying, "I could have given you the statistics on how people rate typical customer service on a day-to-day basis, but this is even better, because it has *face validity*—meaning the whole room is pretty much saying it." Then ask them, "What would be in it for us, our team or our organization, if people rated us a 9 or a 10?" Faces brighten; they all get fired up.

Walk them through a negative and a positive customer service experience. You could ask, "What is your experience with horrible customer service?" As they share their experience, they articulate the characteristics of horrible service right away. Next, you ask, "What is your experience with really good customer service? What makes customer service excellent?" Then you have them consolidate characteristics of great customer service, and use those characteristics to introduce your fabulous customer service model. By using this strategy, you are creating face validity or believability and enhancing the immediacy of their buy-in.

The act of remembering an early experience connects learners to the concepts in the new model. This personally links and inspires their own neural connections and realizations, and brings them to the surface. This cycle of connecting to an experience and having a realization has to happen in more than one way. You want it to happen over and over. In this way, the learners are coming up with the new knowledge you are trying to teach as you are teaching it. They become your partner in the learning, and they experience meaningful epiphanies—aha moments. These insights are powerful; they strengthen retention.

Link Pre-Work to Key Concepts and Practice

After people experience and then label the content, follow up with an activity in which they practice or teach key concepts. If you gave a pre–learning event assignment, this is a good time to link that work with a new activity. Participants may have read an article, done an assessment, or answered study guide questions for a book. They can use those to identify and teach key concepts. They can quiz each other, work through a crossword puzzle, create a mind map, or do any other strategy where they actively use that information.

Provide Context and Share Research

Now that you've introduced or initially explained your model, pause and share the validity—the research—for the 50 percent of your class who are analytical and want this concrete information before fully committing. Even though you may have generated some stats from the research earlier, they will want to know more information, such as: What is the basis of your model? What is the history, and what are the data? What beliefs drove it? What research led you to create this model? They will want to know more about you, the author of the model, and how the idea came about. This information gives more analytical people a foundation for listening and connecting, because the model is based on research rather than random theory. It is important to have good, solid research to back up your material and opinions; this will give the participants more confidence and a greater willingness to trust and engage with you.

In our *TrustWorks*[2] program at Blanchard, Cynthia Olmstead, the author, shares the purpose of the program—"to understand the impact of trust within the workplace and learn a language to enhance sustaining, trusting relationships." This is how she does it:

1. She talks about "what trust is" while gathering information on trust enablers and trustbusters from the learners' own experiences.

2. She then shares that trust is the core issue impacting organizational team and leadership effectiveness, citing research from such sources as the Stanford Symposium on Trust, Tom Peters, Warren Bennis, Stephen Covey, Peter Drucker, and *Harvard Business Review.*

3. She explains the global impact of trust on strategic partnerships, outsourcing, and the global economy, as well as the need for flexible, committed teams.

4. She shares that in one study 99 percent of employees surveyed considered trust to be the most important criterion in the workplace today, with only 39 percent of employees saying they trust the senior leaders, and only 20 percent trusting the organization they work for.

5. She shares a survey of 2 million workers at 700 companies that found the length of an employee's stay is largely determined by his or her relationship with the boss.

6. She then explains how trust impacts turnover, and more.

7. After sharing the evidence of the power of trust, she has learners go to flip charts and label their thoughts on trust builders and eroders by using the model she has created for how to build trust.

This background rallies people to say, "Wow. Trust is so important to my organization. I had better sit up and pay attention."

Put a New Twist on Interactive Lectures and Demos

Lectures, if done correctly, can capture the attention of learners and inspire them to do the hard work of embedding new learning into practice. A lecture should utilize some or all of the following:

Orienting: Keep key points relevant and up front so participants can track what you are talking about.

Handouts: Most people appreciate some kind of handout that has a place to write a clear synthesis of key points or places to fill in the blank, which actually enriches participation.

Descriptions: Concepts, objectives, principles, or steps are clearly described.

Stories: Stories touch the emotional center of the brain and cause the switch to go on that releases chemicals that not only cement learning but say, "Hey, this is important. Pay attention." Stories also bring out the heart of the content.

Research: Clear, enthusiastic explanations of content include the underlying research for that content, which builds credibility, relevance, and validity.

Variety: Vary where you stand, the gestures you use, visuals you cue up, printed materials you hand out, types of questions you ask, manipulative materials you use for exercises, and types of activities. All this variety stimulates energy and refocuses the brain.

E	• Energize Learners
N	• Navigate Content
G	• Generate Meaning
A	• Apply to Real World
G	• Gauge and Celebrate
E	• Extend Learning to Action

Visuals/materials: Lectures augmented by posters, paintings, slides, videos, films, podcasts, and movies add a new dimension and enable optimal learning due to multiple modalities. Color-coding different sections of your content increases memory as the brain hooks each concept to a color tag to assist in identifying objects or ideas that belong together.

Transitions and links: Making clear transitions from one topic to the next increases the amount of neural connections made in the brain, thus improving retention and reducing the amount of time it takes for the brain to switch from one topic to another. Too much time with the brain switching topics can cause ocular lock, where participants are looking at you but have actually glazed over and may be completely lost. All they'll be hearing, like in a Charlie Brown cartoon, is, "Waa-wa-waa-waa-wa-waa."

Giving directions: One of the areas I consistently see inexperienced people get tripped up on is the area of giving directions. Very often a teacher will stand in front of the room and give everyone three or four things to do: first do this, then do that, then do this, then do that, and then you're done. I recommend that you have directions clearly written somewhere and that you give those directions explicitly, one step at a time, stopping between each step to make sure everyone is with you. Give direction for the first step or part of the procedure; wait for people to do that activity; then pause. Give directions for doing the next part; wait a little while before moving on. Check in with people after each step in the procedure. After giving clear direction for the entire procedure, immediately walk around and check in to be sure everyone understands and is capable of following the procedure. Walk the people who are having difficulty through a few examples until they get it. Always give a learner another way of looking at something if one way isn't working. Stating directions simply and clearly, and getting people off to a great start enables greater success and builds confidence.

Behavioral modeling examples and demonstrations: Clear, concrete, vivid examples or demonstrations of what you are talking about or what you want participants to do give their brains an image of the effective behavior and a picture of a good job. Since the brain stores in images not words, these images transfer the learning to doing at a greater acceleration. Early on, as you navigate your content, an effective strategy is to model what you would like your participants to do. Demonstrating effective practices enables people to see the desired end state.

Video/DVD examples: Another aspect of a lecture could be a video or DVD example of what a good job looks like, enabling people to observe someone else verbalizing the specific new behaviors or demonstrating the new skill.

Summary: End with a summary of key ideas and a challenge to move those ideas to action as well as key commitments so participants have a target to work for.

Lectures work well when combined with interactivity such as small and large group discussions, flip chart activities, oral/written journaling or reflecting, videos, and other stimulating activities.

Expand Connections with Case Studies

A variety of examples come to mind when someone says, "Let's do a case study." Very often, people think of *Harvard Business Review* when they think of a case study. These are in-depth analyses of a real issue that an organization has, along with expert feedback on the issue. Typically, in a meeting or workshop, you would want to do a smaller case study and use a strategy for giving someone a brief analysis of a situation where a person is doing the task relevant to what you are teaching. For example, if you are teaching a sales strategy in which a salesperson uses deep product knowledge with a client, a case study would describe someone in that situation working with a client and sharing product knowledge and competitor analyses, and teams would analyze what the person did well and what he might have done differently.

A case study is a great tool for giving learners practice recognizing your model. You could give them a written case study depicting only appropriate behaviors, then ask participants to pull your model out of the example and show where it followed what you wanted people to do. This enables people to apply the principles that you have been grappling with and discover new connections as they analyze the situation.

You can use case studies or mini-scenarios with your model to challenge learners to determine what they would do in a particular situation. For example, if you were teaching listening skills, you might show a photo or a video illustrating a situation in which people weren't listening, then the participants would analyze what they would do differently to be a better listener. Occasionally I have the participants write their own mini–case studies and give them to other groups to analyze using the new information or model.

CHAPTER 5 • STEP 2: NAVIGATE CONTENT

E • Energize Learners
N • Navigate Content
G • Generate Meaning
A • Apply to Real World
G • Gauge and Celebrate
E • Extend Learning to Action

Models on posters drive focus and activities.

Build Repeatable Success with Skill Practice

Role-plays—or *skill practice* as I call it for the people who have an aversion to role-plays—are situations where you have participants actually perform the new skill as they are learning it. They practice it with their job aids, specific guidelines, or possibly even scripts, and they get feedback from each other on how they did.

Provide a One-Page Synthesis or Job Aid

You need to create a one-page job aid that says what your model is and how people can use it. This shows your key concepts on a 5×7 or 8½×11 card, and it helps learners see a synthesis of all the pertinent content they'll be using as they move forward in the learning session. You want them to use that job aid and to have it be the core of your program and practices. Think of it as a power tool and integrate it with the activities you facilitate. It is called a job aid because it helps people do their job.

In Chapter 3, Figure 3.3 shows the ENGAGE Model job aid. Another example would be the THRIVE Model explained in Chapter 2 and its job aid shown in Figure 2.1.

Teach to Diverse Learning Styles

Everyone has his or her own learning style or preference. These different styles are not better or worse; they are just different. If you teach me in a way that focuses on my learning style, it will be a lot easier for me to learn. This means that I favor a particular way of taking in, processing, and manipulating information, but you might learn best in a different way.

When children are very young, you often see evidence of learning style preferences as you observe them and notice the kinds of toys and activities they gravitate toward. Adults do the same thing: they gravitate toward activities that align with their natural learning style. That's why some people like to read, do crossword puzzles, and watch news broadcasts, while others can't get enough of listening to talk radio, books on tape, or music on their iPod, and still others like to play Nintendo Wii games or go rock climbing.

Most people learn in multiple ways using visual, auditory, and kinesthetic cues. But everyone has a dominant style. Visual learners will love the posters on the walls, and they will like making their own images. Auditory learners do well with recordings and discussions. And kinesthetic learners want to touch everything and move around a lot—they like to build and draw pictures. When you are working with one individual, it is wise to learn that person's particular learning style and exploit it to their advantage. For example, if visual images are powerful for that person, use them in multiple ways to embed learning. When working with groups, or even with some individual learners, the more you tap into all three learning modalities, the more you are helping learners achieve greater depth and breadth of learning.

How Do You Best Learn?

Let's discuss your own learning preference, as it has implications for how you choose to teach or interact with others. (*If you have not yet taken the Building Excellence Profile, now would be a good time to do so. See Resource A for how to access this great assessment which will share with you 28 elements for maximizing learning and retention.*)

Visual.   When you are learning (or living your life), do you make a lot of lists? Do you enjoy images, pictures, and dialogue? If you're trying to spell a word, do you visualize it? Do you remember people's faces? Are you good at reading and following instructions? Do you write things down a lot and enjoy a neat, orderly environment?

E	• Energize Learners
N	• Navigate Content
G	• Generate Meaning
A	• Apply to Real World
G	• Gauge and Celebrate
E	• Extend Learning to Action

You are a visual learner. Your brilliance might be brought out when someone allows you to take a lot of notes or gives you a chance to preview books and articles before reading them by looking at all the pictures and the table of contents. You may enjoy sitting more toward the front of a room to better see what's going on. You might like using a colored highlighter and different colored pens to create your mind map and visual cues of what you just learned. You may feel more energized in a room where there are pictures and images on the wall.

Auditory.   If you are struggling with something, do you call someone so you can talk it out? Do you enjoy listening to lectures? Do people suggest that you write things down? Do you talk to yourself? Do you enjoy music? Do you repeat people's names so you remember them? Do you find yourself singing in the car? Do you enjoy learning in a very quiet environment because sound can sometimes interfere with your ability to learn? Do you talk through steps of something as you are trying to help it flow?

You are an auditory learner. You prefer to hear information through spoken explanation. You are distracted by noise, but you learn by listening and sharing with others. Auditory learners not only like to hear other people's voices, they like to hear their own voice. People with an auditory preference like to have time to share their thoughts and repeat important information aloud. They enjoy audio files or podcasts and listening to lectures. They enjoy making up songs about information or discussing what's being learned.

Kinesthetic.   Do you like to get up and move? Stand at a flip chart? Walk as you think out your ideas? Do you take a lot of notes or doodle? When someone is teaching you something, do you prefer that you get a chance to try it and manipulate it? If you are learning to use new expense-management software, instead of listening to the flow and watching, would you rather have them let you just do it so you can get the key concepts? Do you remember the emotions of what happens with someone more than some of the details? Do you typically want to figure things out yourself or write things down to see if they are right? Do you want to be involved with the content?

You are probably a kinesthetic learner. You like to learn hands-on and try things yourself. If someone is showing you their vacation pictures, you actually want to touch the vacation pictures and you want to be the one who flips through them. You love touch-technology, because you learn by doing. You memorize by walking, flipping through flash cards, and building concepts and connections.

Kinesthetically experiencing a dendrite.

Maximizing learning for kinesthetic learners means allowing them to move and helping them rewrite concepts, mind maps, and flowcharts. Kinesthetic learners do best when their muscles are moving, stimulating the brain and releasing the chemicals that create the neural connections. Kinesthetic learners often like comfortable seating and lighting. They enjoy creating models, standing, walking, and talking. They like activities like Think/Pair/Share, where you sketch out your ideas and then get up and walk with someone for 10 minutes and explain the ideas to them while you are walking. Enabling them to act out information, meaning, and interpretation creates a space where they naturally take in information. Kinesthetic learners come up with their brilliance as they *move* and *do*.

One last note about kinesthetic learners: Often it's more difficult for them to tell you what they are going to do. They would prefer to just do it, hone it, and then tell you what they did and come up with solutions through demonstration.

E	• Energize Learners
N	• Navigate Content
G	• Generate Meaning
A	• Apply to Real World
G	• Gauge and Celebrate
E	• Extend Learning to Action

Learning Style Strategies		
Visual Learners	**Auditory Learners**	**Kinesthetic Learners**
• Show three-dimensional objects. • Tell vivid stories with descriptive words where people can create pictures. • Use color, peripherals, and pictures in the room. • Use imagery where they create a vivid picture. • Use mind maps so they are looking at a graphic instead of words.	• Listen to teacher or someone else talk. • Listen to themselves by reading to a group. • Paraphrase to a partner information they just learned. • Create a recording of what they are reading so they can play it back. • Use stories that embed the learning. • Think/pair/share-think about something, then pair up with someone and share it with them. • Practice a skill and then describe to a partner what they are actually doing as they are doing the skill. • Make a song, a rap, or a mnemonic.	• Take notes. • Build models. • Create pictures or images of written words. • Role-play or act out a process. • Assimilation. • Interview people about the topic. • Teach others in the class. • Be the one to create the test from the content, and give it to others to try to learn from it. • Get up and move to a flip chart.

Figure 5.1. Learning Style Strategies

We All Have Multiple Intelligences

Howard Gardner, psychologist and professor of neuroscience from Harvard University, challenged conventional definitions and measurements of intelligence with his Multiple Intelligence Theory.[3] Just like we take in information better in one way over another, we all are "smarter," or more intelligent, in one or more ways over others. Our strongest intelligences drive our ultimate success in life. Gardner explained in the 1983 publication of his theory that there are not just two intelligences—linguistic and logical mathematical, commonly associated with IQ on which intelligence is often assessed—but actually eight intelligences (he has since added a ninth: Existential Intelligence).

In learning situations, often our intelligence is assessed or evaluated on how well we answer questions or how well we can read or listen to new content, answer questions about it, and take tests on it. Dr. Gardner says that life's gifts show up in the form of "multiple intelligences," which create opportunities for people to be smart in a variety of ways.

This bears significantly on teaching methods and career development. In order to give every learner the opportunity to be successful, the teacher must figure out not how smart people are, but *how* people are smart. You do this by tapping into the intelligence that may be their strength, and make sure that throughout your presentation, whether it's a short meeting or a two-day workshop, you utilize a variety of exercises to tap into a variety of intelligences, enabling all to be smart.

How Intelligence Shows Up.   People can be naturally smart in many ways. Using Dr. Gardner's categories, let's look at how gifts show up in people's interests and preferred learning styles.

Intrapersonal: These are self-reflecting people who know themselves very well. They have a great desire to reflect on what they believe and think. They like to keep journals.

Interpersonal: These people are "people smart." They love social experiences, interacting with others, sharing their thoughts and listening to the thoughts of others, and helping people solve problems. They remember every detail related to the people in their world.

Verbal/Linguistic: People with this type of intelligence have a love of words. My son can spend hours researching the origin of words and has had a love of writing and reading since even before he went to school.

Naturalist: These learners like going on a little walk or sitting outside. They can remember every plant and every bird. If you have any images to post or project, you may want to include images of nature. That will make these learners feel comfortable and more connected.

Visual/Spatial: These people like to look at things and are smart because they can create images as well as analyze images. They are the ones who love it when your PowerPoint has pictures instead of just words.

Logical/Mathematical: Numbers-oriented learners like analyzing graphs and using logic.

Bodily/Kinesthetic: People who are kinesthetically intelligent are athletes or physically oriented people who enjoy moving around and using their bodies. They are good at manipulating information. They like touching and manipulating objects and grasping concepts in a

E • Energize Learners
N • Navigate Content
G • Generate Meaning
A • Apply to Real World
G • Gauge and Celebrate
E • Extend Learning to Action

learning experience. They like to create flow charts and move things around, literally, with large muscle movement.

Musical/Rhythmic: These people enjoy putting something to music, making a song about something, or having material put to a song.

Existential: These individuals enjoy thinking about and questioning, and are curious about life, death, and ultimate realities.

Figure 5.2 on page 96 provides exercises that enable people to shine by using their greatest intelligence.

Use Engaging Teaching Strategies

Lecture Like a Star

Many effective strategies have participants actively involved with new content. That said, the lecture or keynote approach, where you stand up and present your content with a vibrant PowerPoint deck, does have its place and can be used effectively to a degree. Lectures also can be useful for pre-learning or follow-up. Marcus Buckingham, the exciting speaker and co-author of *Now, Discover Your Strengths*, delivers, as a follow-up to a keynote address, an outstanding talk on strengths with a PowerPoint deck that you can see on his Web site.[4] Keith Ferrazzi, a renowned expert in professional relationship development and author of *Never Eat Alone* and *Who's Got Your Back*, also offers on his Web site excellent examples of presentations on specific topics relating to his inspiring works on developing lasting relationships.[5] Both of these speakers link their content and ideas to pivotal issues that people commonly experience. They create strong emotional connections to strengths and relationship building (i.e., their content) through sharing a variety of powerful, persuasive graphics, stories, and data. It's worth visiting these Web sites to see these brilliant men in action, delivering their lectures.

Mind Mapping and Other Graphic Organizers

There are times when you can blend strategies. You can augment a lecture by having participants fill out a purposeful worksheet or by having them recognize and check things off on their job aid. You could create a linear outline in which you leave parts blank for them to fill in. These are called *graphic organizers.* Graphic organizers are designed to activate prior knowledge and help ready participants for the new information. Sometimes they are sent out ahead of time and draw information about the content people are about to experience; other times, they are used in class to help

Intrapersonal	• Inner self-knowledge • Self-awareness • Learning logs • Self-assessment • Response journals • Goal setting • Portfolios • Reflecting • Interpreting • Inventing • Creating
Interpersonal	• Working with others • Charismatic leaders • Oral expression • Caring for/comforting others • Communicating with others • Group activities • Team tasks • Partner work • Interview
Verbal/ Linguistic	• Metaphors/similes • Storytelling • Language • Literacy • Reading • Writing • Speaking • Listening • Books • Poetry • Essays • Speeches • Dialogues • Conversation • Guest speaker
Naturalist	• Predicting • Relating • Nature • Categorizing • Plants • Flowers • Animals • Seashells • Synthesizing classification of wildlife • Nature walks
Visual/Spatial	• Games • Puzzles • Describing • Dreaming • Illustrations • Film • Cartoons • Paintings • Maps • Imaging/ visualizing • Visually depict information and ideas • Video
Logical/ Mathematical	• Recording • Collecting • Abstract reasoning and thinking • Principle • Debating • Calculating • Coding, comparing • Judging, proofs • Concluding • Problem solving • Logical arguments • Theory • Computing
Bodily/ Kinesthetic	• Body Mnemonic • Manifested in muscle memory of body • Hands-on learning • Movement • Manipulative • Labs • Role playing • Constructing • Drama • Practicums
Existential	• Pondering fundamental questions of existence • Meaning of life and death • Considering ultimate realities • Philosophical • Religious theory • What is love? • Where does humankind fit in the big picture? • Abstract theories of existence

Figure 5.2. Activities for Multiple Intelligences

E	• Energize Learners
N	• Navigate Content
G	• Generate Meaning
A	• Apply to Real World
G	• Gauge and Celebrate
E	• Extend Learning to Action

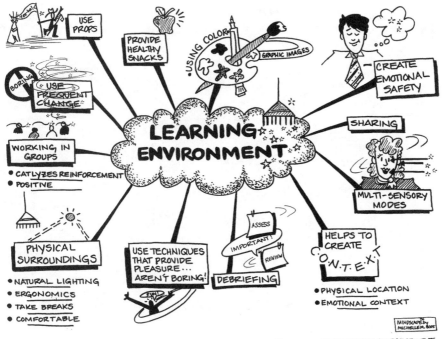

Figure 5.3. Example of Mind Map on Creating an Optimal Learning Environment

people keep graphically organized as they fill in the blanks throughout a presentation.

You might engage learners in doing a mind map (see Figures 5.3 and 5.4). These can be very interesting, stimulating, and fun. You can stylize these in different ways, but they serve the same purpose.

Mind mapping is a strategy to help people organize their thoughts in much the same way that their brain processes thoughts. It's one page that holds all the information and concepts around a big idea, such as your content topic. Tony Buzan's research on mind maps demonstrates the advantages of creating mind maps.[6]

- Creates patterns for the brain.
- Organizes ideas by chunking interrelated ideas.
- Helps people see the relationships between topics.
- Boosts recall.
- Helps people make better decisions.

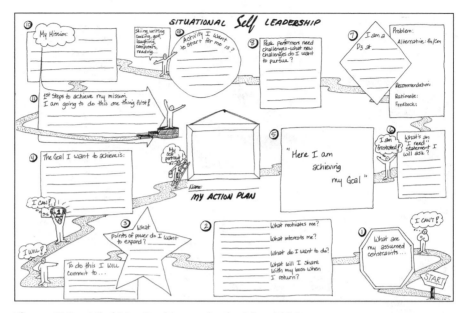

Figure 5.4. Mind Map Serving as a Synthesizing Activity

- Enables increased retention.
- Integrates the left and right brains.
- Integrates the brain biology and the mind's psychology, thus deepening learning.

Here's how it works. In the center of the mind map is the core topic. Branching off are subtopics. Extending from those branches are details of the subtopics. Ask learners to use pictures on their mind maps, as the brain stores in images, not words. To strengthen the connections and differentiate topics, you can color code different concepts.

Modeling

"Show, don't tell" is a well-known rule for writers and an effective strategy for teaching. There are several ways to model concepts you want learners to understand. Showing a short video of the concept in action and having participants deconstruct the information you're trying to teach from the video is a way to inspire their passion to learn and show what a great job looks like. If you are teaching people to coach, you might have them watch a video of a great example of someone coaching an individual who is resistant to change. In larger teams, in pairs, or individually, the learners then

E	• Energize Learners
N	• Navigate Content
G	• Generate Meaning
A	• Apply to Real World
G	• Gauge and Celebrate
E	• Extend Learning to Action

deconstruct what they've seen and heard in the video in terms of the coaching model. You ask questions to prompt them through the exercise. "What did you notice the coach doing to help the coachee not just understand the new behaviors, but to actually own his role and take responsibility for changing behaviors while maintaining a positive relationship?"

If you are highly proficient at "doing" what you're teaching, another way to teach a key concept is to model it in front of the room. For example, when teaching a listening model, you could have a conversation with someone in the front of the room, then have people use their job aids to label which parts of the EAR Model (Explore, Acknowledge, Respond) they have just seen in action.

One final way to model is to demonstrate what you are teaching throughout your class. For example, if I teach customer service, I walk around picking up cups, plates, or anything else I can think of in order to demonstrate serving others.

Interactive Conversations

Talking—actually saying ideas out loud—is a great way to work out your understanding of ideas. You can give participants a short article (one to three pages) or a chapter of a book, or have them watch a video. Then they can discuss the content at their table, tying it to the new content presented. The interaction can stop there, or you can have one person at each table take notes and record the group's key ideas in their discussion. Ask all the people, except the recorder, to disperse to other tables for additional discussion on the same topic. The recorder remains at the original table to relate the ideas of her previous group. Depending on how much time you have, you can do a few rounds of this kind of discussion.[7]

> Using different senses activates different parts of the brain.

Cooperative Learning and Jigsaws

Peer-to-peer teaching or cooperative learning is another way to interact with new content and work through concepts. You can do this using an article or book chapter as the stimulus. Instead of having a discussion, individuals in the group take turns teaching the concepts. If you use a three-page article, you could take groups of three and give person A page 1, person B page 2, and person C page 3. Each person reads his or her page, and then they teach each other what they have learned. They can use their job aid, flip charts, or any tools that work for them.

In my learning organization class at the University of San Diego, I use an activity that I call the Jigsaw, along with a paper written on the topic of *action learning.* Action learning is a strategy used to gain organizational intelligence by involving employees in the process of solving their own problems. As issues arise, cross-functional teams are formed who determine areas where the group needs to get smart *before* they try to solve the problem. After they all get smart on their individual topics, they come back together to build everyone's knowledge on aspects of the topic and *then* try to use that information with their ideas and experience to solve the problem. The paper I use for the Jigsaw activity in class describes three different examples of action learning used in three organizations. In groups of three, students each read one part of the article—metaphorically, one piece of the puzzle—and then come together in groups of three (one from each article) to share their piece of the puzzle and teach each other the examples, strategies, and powerful organizational outcomes of action learning from the three organizations. They are free to teach in whatever style is natural for them. This is a great way to have them become an expert in one aspect of the article so there is greater receptivity to the other learning.

The Ken Blanchard Companies used a Jigsaw with the staff of the San Diego Padres to teach the values of safety. Guest services personnel were shown how to teach themselves the values using a model that included presentations on safety to groups of 15 people. They broke into three groups of five, obtained all the information they needed to teach, and they taught it back to the other two groups. Think of how much better they learned than if they had just sat listening to someone talk about the three safety issues!

The strategies in this section and many other examples throughout the book incorporate the principles that maximize learning and drive future application of the content. Combined with the Brilliance Learning System principles and practices for fostering the most effective teaching and learning, these techniques for interacting with the core concepts will help your learners acquire information, learn skills, problem solve, and understand concepts.

The frequency of the interactivity is critical. I recommend doing an activity every five to seven minutes when you are in a physical, face-to-face learning session, or every two to three minutes if you are in a virtual session. Make certain your activities are multisensory, playing to the various strengths of everyone in the room, so that you make it highly possible for everyone to experience their brilliance.

Checking for Understanding, and Guided Practice

The third part of teaching your new content offers the learner an opportunity to grapple with the content in a way that checks for and deepens her

E • Energize Learners
N • Navigate Content
G • Generate Meaning
A • Apply to Real World
G • Gauge and Celebrate
E • Extend Learning to Action

understanding and increases her level of mastery under the direct supervision of the teacher. Before proceeding to the application of the content to real-life situations, this part of your session serves to demonstrate to the student that she actually learned the new content—she "got it."

Your goal in this step is to help people practice the concepts correctly the first time, and to make sure that the transfer of new knowledge is effective. It's important that the students have confirmation that they have the knowledge, so that they become fluent in the new language of the content and they can apply it later.

One way of achieving this goal is by having participants teach the new knowledge to others. When people sit and listen to someone else teach, they retain less than when they do the work to actively prepare and teach it to someone else. That's why it is mandatory that your learners are active, not passive, during the majority of the learning session, and that they are teaching, talking, and reflecting as much as possible. If the learning comes from them, through their verbalization and interaction, they have an optimal chance for real learning.

With this in mind, the strategies for checking their understanding and guiding their practice will give participants multiple ways to teach concepts in the new model or to teach the model itself. This is where the revolutionary principle *Whoever is doing the teaching is doing the learning* comes into play, along with the 70/30 Principle—*Learners talk and practice skills 70 percent of the time*. While your learners are interacting, teaching, and actively practicing, your role is to inspire hard work, facilitate learners' success, coach them and guide them, reward them, and remind them of how much they've learned—how brilliant they are.

What follows is a wide variety of methods to ensure you "TIP" the scales of learning with Total Intense Participation.

Out-of-Context Practice.   To ensure people have an opportunity to get the content *before* moving it to the messy real world, it's a best practice to check for understanding of the content *out of context* first. This way, you can control the variables and help people accurately learn the concepts of the content. The multiple variables in a real-world situation challenge the brain to stay clear and focused. The brain has to deal with all the variables around it, even those that have nothing to do with what it is learning, which diffuses the energy of strong neural connections. For example, when I teach Challenging Conversations, I know that it's natural for people to start thinking many things about the person with whom they need to have one of these difficult conversations. These diverse thoughts are distractions. I want them to actually practice the SPEAK Model and get confirmation that they know this content and its language before they practice it in a real world situation. I want my learners to be focused and laserlike in their thinking. I want to set them up for success and give them the chance to know that they have this knowledge. Real-world practice is coming up in Chapter 7, after you generate meaning and create relevancy for the learning in Chapter 6.

Build in Choices.   As you have people practice their new learning, give them options for how to do it. This gives participants the power to choose how they want to wrestle with the information. People like choices; providing them is another way of valuing and respecting the participants, and it motivates them to work harder.

- One person might like doing a lot of short practices, where he is finding information and answering questions.
- Someone else might like to talk with another person and sketch her practice out on a flip chart.
- Someone else might like to watch and analyze a video because he is auditory; a partner could assess his learning by asking questions.
- Other people might like to do it on their own. You could have a couple of computers set up in the room where those who learn independently could go practice online without having to talk with anyone else about it, and there could be an online quiz for them to use.
- Someone might choose to do a mini–case study, role-playing exercise, or skill practice.

Repetition, Repetition, Repetition.   Repetition builds up the neurological network that enables learners to access information when it's time to apply the knowledge in real-world situations. Any exercises for practicing or talking through the concepts and the model are good. Whether you are teaching a sales model, a leadership model, or a customer service model—any model—have your learners practice the steps out of context first. The repeated practice enhances retention and builds confidence, and the stronger neural connections enable better recall.

More Strategies for Out-of-Context Practice.

Four Corners: This is an activity to get people to review key content by walking to a place in the room and standing by the answers. If you have four possible answers, tape those to the wall in four corners. Then ask a question, and have participants go to the location of their choice and discuss the core ideas.

E	• Energize Learners
N	• Navigate Content
G	• Generate Meaning
A	• Apply to Real World
G	• Gauge and Celebrate
E	• Extend Learning to Action

Question/Answer: Asking questions seems like a simple concept, yet rarely do people ask questions in a way that engages learners. (I've been asking questions throughout this book; hopefully I've captured your attention.) How do you do this effectively? (There I go again!) First of all, before you ask a question, make sure you have the attention of all participants. Second, ask a question before calling on someone so that everybody has a chance to try to answer it. Third—and this is the cool part—before calling on someone, wait for 40 to 50 percent of the hands to go up, or read the room and wait until people look at you like they have the answer. Or wait for seven seconds so that more people actually have thought of what the answer is. Typically, I don't call on participants who don't have a hand up or who have not stated that they would like to share—you don't want to make participants feel uncomfortable or humiliated. On the contrary, you want to make them feel the opposite—really safe and supported, and set up for success.

When someone answers a question correctly, what do you do? Good question. You need to take advantage of a teachable moment and explain *why* the answer is correct. Many teachers just restate the answer, but that's not enough. And what if the answer is wrong? *Your job is to help them be smart by directing their thinking to the correct answer, and making them your partner in revealing the correct answer.* You might say, "I'll bet you were thinking . . . and, in this situation . . ." Then restate the question in a way that leads them closer to the correct answer so they end up actually articulating the correct answer themselves.

Scenario Analysis: Design situations where learners analyze different scenarios. You can have participants do mini-lessons, where they teach each other the concepts. These are short and quick, and they can give participants the feel of playing a game.

Think/Pair/Share: Think/pair/share is a three-part exercise where learners *think* about the key concepts they just learned and draw them out on a mind map. People *pair* up, and they can decide if they want to stay where they are or go for a walk—because walking releases norepinephrine and epinephrine, which cement learning. If they choose to walk, they *share* their thoughts while they are walking.

Teach the New Model or Method: Learners get together in pairs. Each learner takes a turn standing up and teaching the other person the concepts in the model. They use their job aid or another tool to explain. You can give them a very short period of time to prepare a mini-teach. They may make a flip chart or sketch out a story that illustrates it, or may choose another strategy. What you want them to do is to take a stab at teaching to a partner what they were just taught. It's typically a short activity, but they partner up for about 5 or 10 minutes and teach each other the model. It can be a 25-minute activity: 5 minutes to prepare, 10 minutes to teach their partner, and 10 minutes for their partner to teach them. It's quick.

Let's imagine I'm teaching Situational Leadership® II (SLII®) to a group of managers. In this model, I want the learners to realize that they have learned to become extremely competent in skills that at one time they could not do. Remember the story exercise, where they wrote what it was like to learn how to drive a stick shift or go skiing? They remembered and wrote about four different development levels, because in SLII® the participants learn that there are four development levels and four leadership styles. They now use their previously written story to teach someone else the SLII® model.

For skiing, David might share, "I started off excited, but I didn't know what to do. I didn't know how to do it. I needed lots of direction." That's D1 (Development Level 1). He points to his job aid to teach his partner. "Then, I found myself face-first in the snow. I wanted to quit; I needed encouragement and more direction." That's D2 (Development Level 2). He points to the job aid again. "Then I was skiing down the slopes." Here's where it goes from learner to doer. "I was really nervous, I was sweating, I was worried, but I could ski and I was zipping along." That's D3 (Development Level 3). He points to the job aid again. The fourth development level, D4, is, "I'm just skiing; I'm good to go now." Through the whole process, David uses his own story and his job aid to teach someone else the key terminology and the SLII® model.

Additional Checking for Understanding and Out-of-Context Practice.

Card Deck Review/Sort: There are many different ways to use different types of card decks. This strategy is quick, engaging, and can review and re-teach in a clear, inviting way. Learners can sort different concepts and put them in different piles; they guess at answers and then turn the card over to see the right answer on the back so they can check their answer right away. For example, if you have four different concepts, write examples on the cards of the four concepts and have participants sort the cards. Let's say you are rolling out a new product and your people will be selling it against three other products. Having participants sort by distinct product features might enhance their recall during their sales presentations. The goal in this card sort is for them to check the right answer instantly so they can correct and then talk about the answer they have

E	• Energize Learners
N	• Navigate Content
G	• Generate Meaning
A	• Apply to Real World
G	• Gauge and Celebrate
E	• Extend Learning to Action

right away. This practice develops strong neurological connections to this new information.

Other Games and Puzzles:

- Concentration game with words that match to the definition.

- Puzzles such as word searches and crosswords.

- Mnemonic to remember core content, that learners can create themselves or you can create for them.

- Games such as bingo, *Jeopardy,* or *Password.* For example, when I taught physical science, and specifically the periodic table, I gave the students a bingo card. I would call out an element, and they would have to find the symbol, such as Au for gold, Ag for silver, or H for hydrogen. They would put a token on the ones they found; when they achieved ELEMENTO, they'd yell out, "ELEMENTO!" to get a "fabulous" prize.

Preassigned Team Presentations: If you have the opportunity to give pre-work before a training class, you may want to give assignments to help people learn a part of your model. For example, at a large financial institution, I trained all their facilitators in powerful learning strategies. Ahead of time, I divided the content into six chunks and gave them core information in packets about the ENGAGE Model. The participants were placed into six teams by the sponsor of the event, and their job for the day of training was to present examples of how they would do their assigned component of the process in their organization with something they were currently teaching. Each team had 30 minutes to present to the group, which enabled people to learn the content. They had to teach the core content I gave them for their section and help the group learn what E was about—how to Energize people, along with their concrete example.

In my Learning Organization class, I give out video case studies by Harvard University's David Garvin.[8] First, the students view the studies. Then, in teams of three and four, they teach the content, make it real through interactive activities, and score each other on their presentations using the score sheet in Figure 5.5.

Navigate with Diversity

Numerous strategies exist for navigating your content. Do not feel limited by the ones in these pages. Keep trying different strategies until you find

Score Sheet for Presentations

I. Content, Thoroughness, and Clarity (10 points)   _____

Full coverage of content—I learned lots!

Demonstrated understanding

Demonstrated relevance to class

Creative/thought-provoking/engaging

Timing (succinct, 25–30 minute presentation)

II. Presentation Style (10 points)   _____

Active class participation (class involved/active versus just sitting and listening)

Tapped into learning needs of auditory, visual, and kinesthetic learners

Use of brain-compatible teaching strategies (music, peripherals, color, hands-on, activated prior knowledge)

Easy to follow (well organized)

Spoken versus read—pulled key learnings *from* students versus told them

III. Handouts/Assessments (5 points)   _____

Handouts were clear, thorough, and easy to follow/helpful (will be something the leaders will use to remind them of great teaching/learning strategies).

Assessment tool/activity/celebration truly assessed what you were trying to teach in your presentation.

Total Points   _____

Comments/feedback/helpful thoughts for how to better maximize learning, or what you want them to continue to do to maximize learning.

_____

_____

Figure 5.5.   Video Case Studies Presentation Score Sheet

the ones you feel work the best for you. It's ideal to be prepared with extras in case you need to change things up or you intuitively sense some learners will do well with a certain type of activity.

As James Flaherty, founder of New Ventures West Coaching and author of *Coaching: Evoking Excellence in Others,* said, "People don't describe what they see, they see what they can describe."[9] This step, Navigate Content, is all about describing, naming, experiencing, and labeling the new content so people see the world differently and, therefore, act differently. The important thing to remember is to teach the content in small chunks and practice, practice, practice so that your participants will connect to the information and be ready to discuss its importance in their lives.

REFLECTION: Review of Chapter 5

REPEATABLE PROCESS FOR NAVIGATING NEW CONTENT, BIG CONCEPT BY BIG CONCEPT

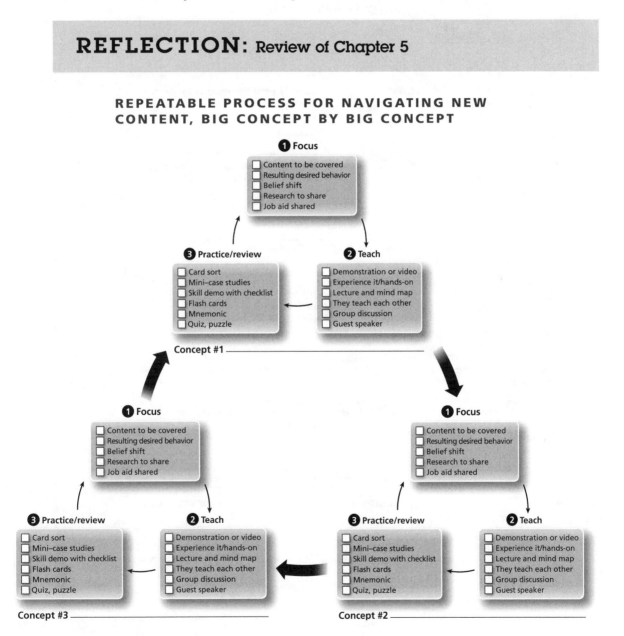

E	• Energize Learners
N	• Navigate Content
G	• Generate Meaning
A	• Apply to Real World
G	• Gauge and Celebrate
E	• Extend Learning to Action

Navigate Content

DO-IT-YOURSELF TEMPLATE

What core information, ideas, and/or takeaways are you hoping to impart?

❑ _____

❑ _____

❑ _____

❑ _____

What research will you share?

_____

_____

What is your opening Total Active Involvement (TAI) idea, question, or activity?

_____

_____

_____

What beliefs do you want participants leaving with to ensure long-term behavior change?

_____

_____

_____

How will you introduce them to the content?

❑ Demonstrate/model
❑ Lecture and slides
❑ Cooperative learning/Jigsaw
❑ Discussion
❑ Guest speaker

❑ Experience, then label
❑ Video/DVD
❑ Written information (handouts)
❑ Stories to share

What activities will help people actively learn, review content, and have Total Intense Participation?

❑ Card sort/matching game
❑ Mind map/graphic organizer
❑ Scenario analysis
❑ Case study
❑ Role-play
❑ Flash cards

❑ Game/puzzle/mnemonic
❑ Multiple-choice/fill-in/true-or-false quiz
❑ Participants teach each other
❑ Think/pair/share
❑ Mini-teach
❑ Video analysis

VISUAL

❑ Images versus work
❑ Color/images
❑ Vivid stories
❑ Mind map
❑ Job aid/one-page synthesis

AUDITORY

❑ Talk with a partner
❑ Describe flow
❑ Recording/podcasts
❑ Listen to lecture/discussion

KINESTHETIC

❑ Puzzle with manipulatives
❑ Flip chart activity
❑ Building the model
❑ Four Corners review (answers in four corners)
❑ Teach a partner

E	• Energize Learners
N	• Navigate Content
G	• Generate Meaning
A	• Apply to Real World
G	• Gauge and Celebrate
E	• Extend Learning to Action

Navigate Content

DO-IT-YOURSELF TEMPLATE

What story/stories will you tell that will tap into emotions and ignite interest about the concept?

_____

_____

_____

MULTIPLE INTELLIGENCES: Help People BE Smart

Verbal/Linguistic
- ❏ Stories
- ❏ Retelling key themes
- ❏ Reading case study
- ❏ Demonstrating

Visual/Spatial
- ❏ Images/charts/posters
- ❏ Building a model/visual depiction
- ❏ Illustrating

Interpersonal
- ❏ Peer teaching
- ❏ Team activities
- ❏ Cooperative learning

Intrapersonal
- ❏ Reflection time/journaling
- ❏ Personal action planning/goal setting

Musical/Rhythmic
- ❏ Creating a song with the topic
- ❏ Musical welcome and while working

Bodily/Kinesthetic
- ❏ Hands-on experiments
- ❏ Arranging puzzle pieces
- ❏ Role-play/skill practice

Logical/Mathematical
- ❏ Visual charts, data
- ❏ Experimentation
- ❏ Coding or sequencing information

Naturalist
- ❏ Pictures of nature in slide
- ❏ Walking outside for 10 minutes of teach/share

Existential
- ❏ Discussing how small learnings fit into bigger picture
- ❏ Philosophical discussions

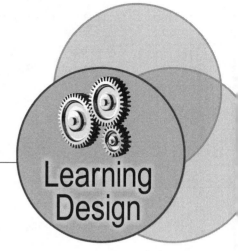
Learning Design

CHAPTER 6

Step 3: Generate Meaning

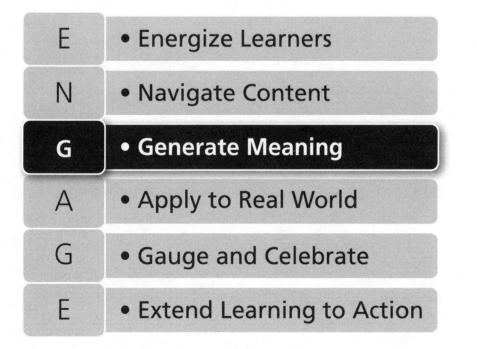

E	• Energize Learners
N	• Navigate Content
G	• **Generate Meaning**
A	• Apply to Real World
G	• Gauge and Celebrate
E	• Extend Learning to Action

Learning is a relationship—a relationship between you, the learners, the content, and the meaning it has for people in their lives. This step of the instructional design is the trigger for confirming the relevancy and the desire to move the learning to action. Your goal is to help your learners articulate the compelling reason to *choose* to act on their learning and transfer it to long-term retention and behavior. This chapter will show you how to encourage people to commit to and clearly state the meaning of the new content in their lives.

In May 2010, I spent three days at the annual American Society for Training and Development (ASTD) International Conference, and I presented the ENGAGE Model during one of the learning sessions. A week after the conference, I received an e-mail from the dynamic Kevin Eikenberry, author of *Remarkable Leadership,* asking me to reflect on the importance of what I had learned from ASTD. Basically, he was helping me to reengage with all I had learned by reminding me of its importance. His message was a catalyst for me to take out my notes from my conference bag, reflect on their meaning in my day-to-day world, and get moving on the commitments I made when inspired by the speakers I had heard.

The objective of generating meaning is to help people be more purposeful during the application process. Articulating the meaning and relevancy helps them come to this realization of their purpose. This step builds confidence and engenders a deep desire to continue to be invested and curious.

It is important that you do not tell them the meaning for their lives.
They need to decide the meaning.

Active versus passive learner:

Active:	Passive:
They tell you the meaning.	You tell them the meaning.

Which is more powerful?
Them telling you.

E	• Energize Learners
N	• Navigate Content
G	• **Generate Meaning**
A	• Apply to Real World
G	• Gauge and Celebrate
E	• Extend Learning to Action

Prime the Brain

Our brain is like a switchyard. The train (information) comes down the track and can go two ways. If we deem the information important, it goes down the track of long-term retention and commitment for future use. If we deem it nice to know, but not worth the energy to embed it into memory, we send it down a different track. To ensure that your great content goes to the part of your learners' brains where long-term retention takes place, people need to see and believe the relevancy and meaning of it. Otherwise, your content just gets filtered out along with the hundreds of less important bits of information they see and hear. The brain asks, "Is this something important?" It may be interesting, but if it has no meaning, we pay it little attention. Therefore, you want to make certain that you are frequently helping learners drill down on "What is the meaning of this learning in my life?"

It is important that you do not *tell* learners the meaning; they need to *choose*—to determine the meaning for themselves. They need to own it. Choosing makes the meaning more powerful.

Endorse Intentions

In addition to the decisions learners make at this stage to act on their intentions, *your* endorsement of this decision increases the probability that they will make the changes needed to break firmly rooted patterns of behavior. Linking these endorsements to the learners' deeply cherished values will also increase the likelihood of change. For example, someone tells you he would like to be clearer about his goals. You ask, "How might that be beneficial to you?" and he says, "So I could be clearer about what I should be working on and simultaneously what I shouldn't be working on." You can then follow up with a question such as "How might knowing what you should be working on, and having clarity about what you don't want to be focusing on, help you?" His response will most likely be linked to his deeply held values, and he might say, "So I could have more time with my family." Now *that* is a reason to change.

To generate meaning, take learners back to objectives to remind them of their goals. "What was the most important concept you wanted to learn in this session? Why did you want to learn it? Why was it important to you? What have you learned that will help you the most in achieving your goals?" Learners are now most likely in the cognitive dissonance stage—the "So what? What does this mean in my life?" stage. They have learned your model and labeled it, and they know, for example, the new sales process or the new leadership model. Their subconscious minds are analyzing the importance of the new content, so this step brings it out in the open and leverages the energy of the community. Learners are searching out the meaning of the content within the context and priorities of their lives.

That is exactly what you want them to do. *Generating meaning is an interlude where you ask them to think about what they've learned and the importance or meaning of that learning in their lives in order to increase the likelihood of change.* As the learner searches, she might think, "I learned there were four stages of development that people go through as they are learning to do a task or goal. What does that mean for me as a leader? It means that, before I learned this, I was labeling *people* as good or bad, capable or not capable, but I never realized that I need to consider the task or goal that a person is working on and their level of development as they work through the four stages. This knowledge is important to me as I seek to bring out the best in all who report to me. As they improve, we all win."

> Generating meaning is an interlude where you ask them to think about what they've learned and the importance or meaning of that learning in their lives in order to increase the likelihood of change.

REFLECTION: Exercise

WHAT'S IMPORTANT?

- Which objective is *most* important to you?
  - Creating dynamic meetings
  - Creating a one-day workshop
  - Creating a two-day workshop
  - Doing a keynote that helps embed your teaching into people's lives
  - Gaining general knowledge of how to design optimal learning experiences

- Now think about *why* this is important for you. How will practicing the ENGAGE Model help you act on the deeply cherished values in your life?

- How will your knowledge of the importance of generating meaning impact your future learning endeavors and make you curious about what is in the rest of this chapter?

Now, dear reader, let's practice. Think about *why* learning the content in this book—learning how to teach in a way that brings out people's brilliance—is important to *you*. Let's start with your objective for reading this book.

Now that you have thought about *why* you need to create meaning and relevancy, there are numerous questions to ask and techniques for learners to do to generate the compelling *why* so that they can make the choice to move their learning forward.

Search for Meaning

You can facilitate the search for meaning through questions and exercises. There are many different ways you can do this. For instance, you can have learners engage in a discussion at their table. Tell them to go around the table taking turns expressing the single most important thing they just learned. Have them follow up immediately by going around again, this time articulating why that learning is important to them. Capture that on a flip chart or on note paper, and have every group report one thing they learned and one reason it's important to them. Alternatively, each group can go to a flip chart and make two columns: column one is what they learned, and column two is why it is important to them.

When I work with new leaders, I use a program called *The Three Keys to Engaging and Energizing People (or How to Help People Thrive in Overdrive)*. It's a fun way to teach leaders how to (1) set clear goals and expectations, (2) develop people, and (3) recognize and reward success. After navigating the content, a question I ask to generate meaning is "What could be the importance to *you* of moving this new learning to action?" I have learners write their responses on a flip chart. Participants write, "I will be more productive," "My group will be more productive," "There will be better teamwork and increased speed to market," "We could retain direct reports who might be thinking of leaving," "I will utilize my time and my employees' time better," or "I can improve my relationships with others."

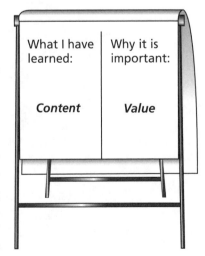

This process helps learners build their commitment by generating meaning, which moves the content to their long-term memory. Writing the benefits and articulating them aloud is a powerful push toward these goals. In addition, they are ratcheting up their belief system and their motivation. In their minds, they are thinking, "Wow! This

Facilitating the search for meaning.

really is something I should act on. Look what it could do for me." They often even say it out loud to one another, and the great synergy is present once again that connects individuals to powerful values and goals, which generates energy to move forward in their learning.

Another reason we want learners to restate and outline the importance of the new information is because the process adds more myelin. In the language of neuroscience, the process of restating learning and articulating benefits means the learner is myelinating the axon to the information—which means releasing the substances that cement learning into their brains.[1] You are helping the learner discover his or her relationship to the new content by linking it to something that previously existed in the brain, something that already has meaning. You ask, "What does it mean?" which connects the learner to previous knowledge. That's what you want, because they have gone deep into the brain to find similar experiences that this information is now zipping over to and saying, "Oh, we're alike. Great. Let's double our bond." It's like one person running down the road grabbing the hand of another person, who runs and grabs the hand of another. Now you have three people hanging onto that information, and there is a much greater chance of that information being retained by the individual.

Create the Value Chain to Change

Human beings have a strong tendency to repeat behaviors that have kept them alive in the past. We might even say we are addicted to or comfortable with our old behaviors, and we are more invested in holding onto them than we are in exchanging them for new, less familiar ones. We are creatures of habit, and even if we *want* to change, we often find it difficult. Research shows that people resist changing even if they really want to change. In *Motivational Interviewing: Preparing People for Change*,[2] authors William R. Miller and Stephen Rollnick describe a scenario where a man who has just had a heart attack refuses to change his eating habits. You would think that this person would be sufficiently motivated to eat better, wouldn't you? Yet, like most of us, he is powerfully attached to his patterns of behavior, perhaps even addicted to them. Without a powerful link to something vitally important to him, such as the vision of his being able to walk with his grandchildren or do some of his favorite things again like hiking or skiing, the probability is high that he will not generate enough self-efficacy to make the change. The degree to which you have your learners envision a clear picture of how the benefits outweigh the cost can explicitly create the value chain to change.

Recruit the Subconscious

As a teacher I am always thinking about what else *I* can do to help learners understand concepts, see the relevancy, and choose to move their learning forward by taking action. A core question that is always present for me is "How can I help the learner come to the realization that this new learning is important?" In *The Learning Brain*, neuroscientist and author Eric Jensen says, "Learning is going on all the time." Referencing Dr. Emile Donchin, who says, "more than 99% of our learning is non-conscious," Jensen states, "That means we simply absorb the experience and our brain adds it to our perceptual maps."[3] Recruiting our subconscious can enhance formal learning strategies and send messages that trigger the learner to choose to take action. Throughout this book, we've talked about many conscious things we can do to create a positive learning environment and value learners. There are strategies we can use to send more subtle messages to learners that this new learning is important and valuable and can make a difference in their world—maybe even help them fulfill their dreams. You might try these strategies to recruit the subconscious to encourage the learner's choice:

- Post student work on the wall. This is a concrete way of saying, "This is important" without actually saying it.

- Share the success stories of well-known, highly regarded people and link their success to the new learning. Identification with others is a strong motivation.

- Tie in some aspect of the content as a great solution to a problem or challenge that a learner brought up earlier in the session.

These strategies and conscious things you do to connect personally with the learners to make them feel valued—calling them by name or praising them for the rigorous work they've done, for their progress, and for taking risks to bring new behaviors into their repertoire—reinforce the importance of what they just learned, and can encourage them to make the choice to move the learning to action.

Create the Commitment to Apply the Learning

Generating meaning and linking that meaning to closely held values gives learners their best chance of acting on the commitment to apply new learning and to follow through with an action plan. By helping learners make the connection and choice, you are generating the energy to create a change.

Many times, people skip this step in the ENGAGE Model because of a lack of time or a lack of clarity about its importance. If you think about it, it is often after a class that aha moments surface, and we realize the importance of new information to our lives. We want to stop people *before* they half-heartedly dive into the application, and give them a chance to recommit to their goals and values.

This step is crucial. It generates neural connections and provides personal meaning and satisfaction. Learners comprehend the relevancy of the new learning and what it can mean in their lives, and they realize how much they just learned. This is great preparation for what comes next. They are fired up and ready to move their learning to practice and apply it in their world.

E	• Energize Learners
N	• Navigate Content
G	**• Generate Meaning**
A	• Apply to Real World
G	• Gauge and Celebrate
E	• Extend Learning to Action

REFLECTION: Exercise

THE VALUE OF GENERATING MEANING

- When was the last time you remember someone helping you to generate meaning regarding your learning?

- What did the facilitation do to help you discover the value of the new concepts in your life?

- What is the importance of this third step of the ENGAGE Model:

  - For you?

  - For your learners?

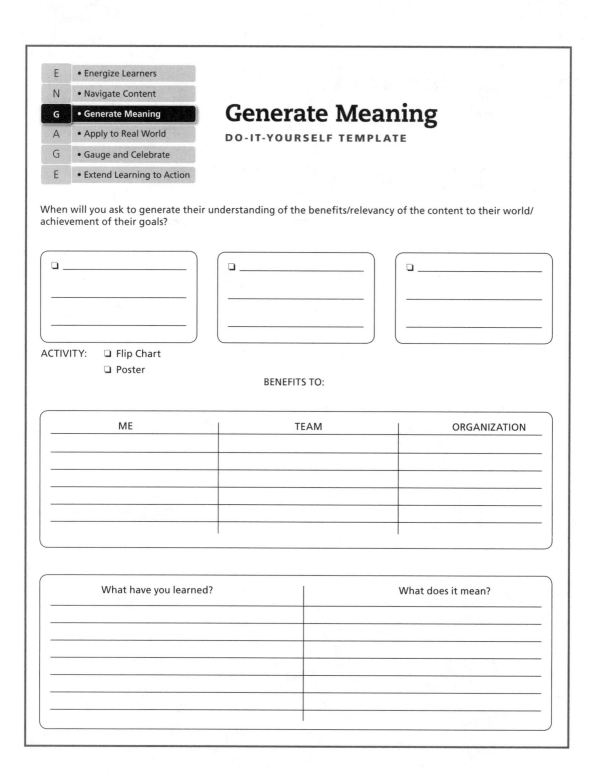

E	• Energize Learners
N	• Navigate Content
G	**• Generate Meaning**
A	• Apply to Real World
G	• Gauge and Celebrate
E	• Extend Learning to Action

Generate Meaning
DO-IT-YOURSELF TEMPLATE

When will you ask to generate their understanding of the benefits/relevancy of the content to their world/ achievement of their goals?

ACTIVITY: ❑ Flip Chart
❑ Poster

BENEFITS TO:

ME	TEAM	ORGANIZATION

What have you learned?	What does it mean?

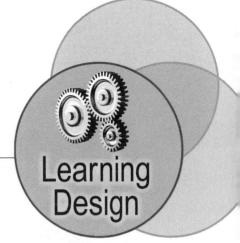

Learning
Design

CHAPTER 7

Step 4: Apply to Real World

E	• Energize Learners
N	• Navigate Content
G	• Generate Meaning
A	**• Apply to Real World**
G	• Gauge and Celebrate
E	• Extend Learning to Action

Congratulations! You've brought your learners through three big steps of the ENGAGE Model, including the crucial one, *Generate Meaning*. You're not quite at the assessing and celebrating step yet, but it's important to take the time to help your learners realize what they have accomplished and to determine how ready they are to apply the knowledge to the work they do (which is piling up while they are at your session).

Many teachers skimp on this step, do it too soon, or leave it out because they don't realize the value of giving ample time for learners to practice using their knowledge in as close to a real-life simulation as possible while still feeling safe and supported by you, their new tools, and their learning community. This is the hard work that many facilitators or teachers know is important, but for sake of time, often expect the learners to do *after* they leave the event. Consequently, the learning seldom transfers into action. This step reverses that. In this step, you help the learner move from knowing to doing, and *you* move from teaching to helping participants apply their learning in the context of their work. In addition, watching learners apply the concepts gives *you* valuable information on how you can improve your content, design, and examples for future use.

Deepen and Retain Key Concepts

I think that you'll agree with me that many people shy away from having difficult conversations. When I teach Challenging Conversations, I use the SPEAK Model, created by Eryn Kalish, conflict resolution specialist, to help people stop avoiding these conversations and confront potential difficulties. Learners do this with a clear strategy and a five-step process for successfully having these conversations. When teaching this, I ask participants to have that needed conversation in real-world practice with a partner and then use a feedback worksheet to see how well they did. I watch people struggle to tell someone the impact of their behavior and/or make a request for a different behavior. It might be a spouse telling his partner that he wants her to be more reliable about picking up their child on time at school because the child gets anxious; or a manager helping someone see the impact on his work and his team of his constantly being late, or letting someone know her work isn't up to par; or an employee asking for a well-deserved raise. All of these conversations are fraught with emotion. Watching people stay mindful and in the part of the brain where they can think, while using the clear model to practice before they leave the class, is a real gift for me and for the participants. It is important to have them actually practice the skill, not just say what they'll do.

In this case, that involves having the learner pretend that their speaking partner is the person they want to have this conversation with and articulating the exact words they want to use, versus saying, ". . . and then I'd tell him . . ." There is so much learning from the witnessing, and from the experience of doing it in a supportive environment. Many times, people are asked to do this final step on their own without guidance and without being in a safe environment, which reduces the chance that the new skill will be put into practice.

> It is important for people to actually practice the skill, *not* just say what they will do.

Lead Up to Real-Life Application

Let's briefly review what has led to the learner's ability to successfully perform a new competence. Before this step, *Apply to Real World,* your learners typically would have done some mini-assessments. They may have watched a video or read a case study, then identified your specific model via those tools. Perhaps they've done a role-playing exercise. In all these strategies, the learner did them as out-of-context practice. They practiced teaching the core concepts so they know what they are, but they didn't have to apply them yet to their real lives. For example, they may know and be able to recognize the steps to effective negotiation, but they haven't thought of the situation where they need to negotiate or actually practiced their new knowledge and skills. Now is time to have them do "in-context" practice. *Remember, the more real-world practice you have them do, the stronger the neural connection will be that will enable them to have success when they are on their own.*

Benefit from Feedback

Before we dive into many different application strategies, let's focus on how to set up the sharing of feedback, which will be an invaluable aspect of this step. Sharing your best thoughts and ensuring they get woven into the practice of the learner benefits both the person practicing using the new competency and the person reviewing the checklist or job aid. To set up the application step, ask yourself what you really want participants to do and how you most clearly and effectively can facilitate effective application practice for learners. *Remember, you want them to model as closely as possible what you would like them to do with your content after they reenter their lives.* Regardless of the content of your model, learners will use the new skill with a partner-observer so they can receive the benefit of feedback, and they will use their job aid or checklist to see if they did everything the model requires.

Feedback Strategy: The SHARE Method

I like my SHARE method because it is easy to remember.

Show the model or job aid and review the ideal performance standards.

Have them (then you) share positives and what they would add next time to improve.

Ask the feedback receiver to share the impact of these additions.

Realistically create agreements for next steps.

Evaluate the benefits of new behaviors and give each other any additional feedback.

Application Strategies

Learning Lab: Mock/Role-Play with Partner. A learning lab is a structured activity for participants to experiment with their learning. Using a specially created template that takes them through a process, they sketch out their thoughts and consider how they want to apply the learning. They decide how to approach and use the model within their work or personal life. After they have identified that, they will use their job aid to sketch out their plan. You need to create very clear, step-by-step templates/worksheets to help them do this. The worksheets may be two or three pages, and will include space for people to write down a statement of a real situation in which they would use the new content. Just like in a science lab, after creating their plan, they begin their experiment by talking with a partner and demonstrating their new skills.

The worksheets or templates also will include a series of questions they will ask each other when they are done with the real work practice. This list or worksheet should have the optimal flow for the situation in order to create a rich conversation about what worked and what didn't.

If you were teaching people to have effective performance management meetings, you might practice this meeting by having each person fill out a worksheet with clear directions about how to have this performance management conversation. The manager decides who he will focus on, lists the person's goals and current development level, and articulates dif-

E • Energize Learners
N • Navigate Content
G • Generate Meaning
A • Apply to Real World
G • Gauge and Celebrate
E • Extend Learning to Action

ferent aspects of the person's role and what that individual needs most from the leader. Then the class participants are told they will practice having these conversations and then debrief using questions such as these:

- Were the goals clear?
- Do you agree that the goals as stated are the best ones for the person to focus on?
- Did the leader listen to the direct report?
- Did the leader give direction that built confidence?
- What type of support did the leader give to build commitment?
- Was a system set up for monitoring performance?
- How was the direct report feeling when leaving the meeting?

Sketching out the conversation is the important next step. If you assigned pre-work before the learning event, you could connect it to the new content at this point during the learning session. Maybe one of the pre-work ideas was to identify someone the learner wants to have a challenging conversation with. After sketching out the performance management conversation, the learner would call the person, actually have the conversation, then come back to the class and report on it. Or if you are doing this training onsite, the designated person could show up, and the conversation could take place face-to-face in a private room.

Cross-Training. Participants determine where they will use the new information on the job. They then partner up with someone from another division and train that person in how to use the new knowledge, ideas, models, or information in that person's department. The benefit of doing this in pairs is that they are bringing the information into their world and simultaneously learning about the world of another person within their organization.

Team Analysis of Application. The analysis activity offers people multiple perspectives on how the learning can be applied. It works well with teams. Standing at flip charts, people analyze how the new content can be applied in different situations. They then travel around the room, writing in their workbooks ideas from other people and their team.

Create Scenarios/Mini–Case Studies. Scenarios help people consider possible applications for future use of the content you are teaching. For example, if your company is initiating a major change and you want to create options for implementation, you might create a variety of scenarios. One group bases their scenario on having all the money in the world to implement the change, and they process what they would do to make it happen. Another group might explore a scenario where it was the greatest initiative ever implemented within their company or team, and then they process how they arrived at the outcomes. This is useful to encourage participants to really think outside the box and consider all sorts of endings and scenarios before actually diving into the planning of how to implement a certain solution. Individuals could create challenging real work scenarios and have other class members try to figure out how to apply the new information/content in those scenarios. Depending on how much time you have, these could be anything from a few paragraphs to a robust case study that others have to analyze. (See www.wildworksgroup.com for more information on scenario building.)

Video Encounter.   Now that small video cameras are relatively inexpensive or in people's phones, they are a viable tool for application practice. There are a lot of ways to do quick videos. You can do this exercise in groups of two or three people. While one participant actually is practicing using the model, a partner videotapes. Then the practicing partner and her buddy or buddies use a series of questions to analyze the practice. The practicing student receives feedback from observers and then does some self-evaluation as they watch the video. Using the job aid or another tool for analysis, learners can see whether they did it the way they wanted to.

In our executive leadership program, we videotape executives explaining their "Leadership Point of View"—the circumstances that have brought them to their moment of leadership and the life experiences that have crafted their behavior. They can watch themselves and ensure that the stories and beliefs about leadership they want to be held accountable for, as well as their own expectations, *sound* like what they had in mind and really hit at an emotional as well as an intellectual level. Doing it this way is much more powerful than if they simply present in front of the group, because the individual has a chance to garner self and peer insight before delivering the message to a team.

Acting Out the Model's Key Concepts.   Another application strategy is to have participants act out the model of your content. In customer service training, the participants act out the touch points a customer might encounter as he or she goes through the complete service experience. For example, in airline travel, touch points with customers are logging online to get the tickets, checking in at the airport and interfacing with the ticket

E • Energize Learners
N • Navigate Content
G • Generate Meaning
A • Apply to Real World
G • Gauge and Celebrate
E • Extend Learning to Action

agent to get a boarding pass or check luggage, interacting with the representative at the gate for a seat assignment change and boarding the plane, interacting with the flight attendant, and going through the baggage claim process. Participants walk through the model to showcase the desired cycle of service and what they want to have happen at each of the touch points or moments of truth.

Skill Practice in a Real Situation.   Skill practice uses role-playing as a strategy. As mentioned before, since some people have an aversion to role-playing, I recommend framing it as skill practice.

You can have participants use this strategy in groups of two or three. If you have created an observation checklist or job aid, participants can use it to act out or role-play in a real situation what you have taught them. As you will see, participants can use it for a variety of scenarios. For example, in a sales seminar, participants could demonstrate product knowledge or have an initial conversation with a buyer. In a coaching workshop, participants could act out a coaching conversation. Place slips of paper in a hat or bowl

Practicing a real-world conversation.

with classic coaching situations written on them, then have participants draw one slip from the hat. If you facilitate management or leadership development seminars, you can use skill practice to help participants learn to manage up, give work direction, or ask for a raise. While one person uses the skills to achieve what he or she wants, the other person plays the role of the client, boss, or direct report. Another way to use skill practice might be in direct client interactions. For example, participants learning a new sales procedure can pretend someone is their client and follow the new procedure from the discovery call and showcasing the new product through overcoming objections and closing.

Action Planning Exercises.   In teams, participants analyze what it would take to move their learning to action in the real world of work or on real problems that currently exist. Together they brainstorm and then share their next steps in order to generate a precise list of possible future actions collected from all participants. This exercise enables them to discuss what obstacles might get in the way of moving their learning to action, what tools they might use to overcome those obstacles, and how those tools will help them act on their best intentions.

Problem Solving.   In groups of three or four, participants pick from a hat a prime example of a situation or problem in which they might find themselves using their new content. These teams have to solve the problem using their new skills and showcase this for the group. They can either act it out or share it orally as a report.

Highly Paid Experts Activity.   Participants in a workshop or people at your meeting write up a situation they are having difficulty with that relates to what is being taught. After 5 to 10 minutes of writing up their situation, they take turns reading their situation aloud and calling on the "Highly Paid Experts," the people in the room, to answer their questions. This can be done in table groups. Usually, I have people number off so they can interact with someone new. This activity also works with smaller groups if you have less time. Or you can ask for volunteers, since some may have better situations where everyone can get involved and do it as a whole group exercise.

Realize the Value of the Knowledge

After the real work practice, you want learners thinking, "That was so cool. Look how much I learned. It was a bit tough to do, but I did pretty well. I got

E • Energize Learners
N • Navigate Content
G • Generate Meaning
A • Apply to Real World
G • Gauge and Celebrate
E • Extend Learning to Action

feedback and know how to improve." Immediately after this practice, you want people to ask themselves, "What would be the value of using this process and skill in my world? What's the benefit to my team, my organization, and myself?" They might think, "I'd have better relationships, improve attention, and people would be engaged." This is what you want. You want people thinking that this is the *best* information they have ever learned, the *best* class they have ever taken, and that it's going to make a huge improvement in their lives. They are firm believers in your brilliant model, and you cement the commitment to continue moving their learning to action. You can point to the flip chart where they wrote their needs or challenges at the very beginning of the session and show how learning the new content enabled them to meet these needs or challenges. This is where you are really having them absorb the value of working to make these new skills part of their daily lives.

Practice New Skills with Observers or Coaches

The next two strategies are most effective when participants do them with a participant-coach, buddy, or participant-witness.

Create a Clear Action Plan

After you have participants practice and apply their knowledge, you will want them to set up very clear action plans. Clarity is important, so emphasize it. In the action plan, participants articulate *clearly and specifically* what their next steps are for using the new content. You want them to target key areas and focus on moving forward. To do this, they need to think about what their strengths are so that they can leverage them and keep doing what they do well. At the same time, you want them to mitigate the things they aren't doing well that might be negatively impacting the people around them or their ability to actually use what they have just learned. This is their opportunity to create a clear learning path for moving forward, once again focusing the brain's energy on their targets.

Create a Support Network

We all know that to act on our best intentions takes incredible effort at times. Creating a support network for people right in the class enables the transfer of learning to action to be dramatically increased. I call this section "insta-coaching," where they get someone who is going to sit down with them and help them see what they want to do differently, how they are going to do it, or what they are specifically going to do moving forward.

Once commitments are made, they are sealed more firmly by setting up a deadline—a "by when." This "by when" inspires the brain's motivation system because it infers a follow-up—accountability. The participant and the new coach decide exactly when they are going to call each other to follow up on whether they have done what they said they were going to do. Maybe they said they were going to have a certain conversation, or they were going to start analyzing their strengths by recording every day what activities they did that strengthened them and what they did that exhausted them. Or maybe they want to use Keith Ferrazzi's example of "pinging" someone, where they are really just reminding people how much they care for them, sending them something they might enjoy, or doing something thoughtful.[1]

Another way to create a support network would be for the group sitting at a table to start a new social networking group online to keep the relationships fresh with the people they have been learning with all day. Creating a group extends the positive emotional bond they've created while learning together and increases the probability of moving learners forward in applying the learning. By helping them create a clear action plan and support network, you are setting them up for success.

Review: Facilitating Application

At this point, you have walked your learners through the first four steps of the ENGAGE Model, and you have moved learning to a new scaffold. You have:

- built confident learners by starting with easier work and moving to more difficult, complex activity.
- modeled what you wanted people to be able to do and encouraged Total Intense Participation.
- used a clear, specific job aid to provide a snapshot of the process and the key concepts.
- used multiple strategies, helping participants succeed through practice with activities for varied learning styles and in a range of contexts.

By now, participants are energized because they know and have practiced a new learning model with a specific language that has meaning to them. They now see something they hadn't seen before. This mutually shared experience for all learners creates a critical mass to move the learning to action. Regardless of the program, if people follow this process, all the learners are actually at the place in their learning where they are ready and willing to act on their best intentions and bring the process into their own lives. They are not only prepared and ready, but they *want* to have that challenging conversation. They know the steps to take when there's a problem in the organization and they really understand the problem. Now they want to *try to solve* the problem.

As you close this part of the learning experience, you may want to ask learners to write down or talk about the various contexts in which they could use their new skills or information in their personal and professional lives. If you listen carefully to their thoughts, you will gain extensive input into their world and find a wealth of ideas or examples to improve your ability to build rapport and have rock-solid content.

REFLECTION: Exercise

MODELING STRATEGY

Think of a skill or a concept you have taught.

- What would be a strategy your participants could use to model, as closely as possible, what you want them to do upon leaving your class or meeting?

- What would be the best strategy to get your participants to *apply* your great content in the exact situation where they will use it?

E	• Energize Learners
N	• Navigate Content
G	• Generate Meaning
A	**• Apply to Real World**
G	• Gauge and Celebrate
E	• Extend Learning to Action

Apply to Real World
DO-IT-YOURSELF TEMPLATE

Skills I want people to apply include:

_____

_____

_____

_____

_____

_____

If people could . . .

❑ _____

❑ _____

❑ _____

❑ _____

❑ _____

. . . after the learning process, it would create optimal results.

To help people apply their learning, I will use the following strategies:

❑ Create a checklist to enable feedback.

❑ Create a learning lab.

❑ Facilitate a cross-training session.

❑ Apply team analysis.

❑ Create a scenario.

❑ Apply a mini–case study.

❑ Record a video encounter.

❑ Act out a system.

❑ Role-play or perform skill practice.

❑ Use an action learning exercise.

❑ Initiate problem solving.

❑ Use a Highly Paid Experts activity.

❑ Create a clear "next steps" action plan.

❑ Create a support network.

To have people show themselves the value of applying the new skills and techniques, I will:

_____

_____

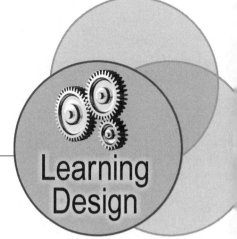
Learning
Design

CHAPTER **8**

Step 5: Gauge and Celebrate

E	• Energize Learners
N	• Navigate Content
G	• Generate Meaning
A	• Apply to Real World
G	**• Gauge and Celebrate**
E	• Extend Learning to Action

Many years ago, when I taught ninth grade physical science, I divided my students into groups, assigned each group a family of the periodic table of elements, and had them come up with a song for remembering that family. They embarked on the song project with relish, including not only the elements but also the characteristics of that family, referencing the number of valence electrons and other details. Fast forward to 2006, when I was at the mall with my sons. Three young men walked up to us and said, "Hey, it's Halsey." They huddled together and began whispering until suddenly, arms around each other's shoulders, they burst into song. I recognized the tune as "California Girls." The words, however, were "The family of alkaline metals really live reactive lives." They cracked up, and so did I, all of us appreciating with amazement that after 20 years, they still remembered the components of the family of alkaline metals because they remembered the song.

When I taught statistics at Chapman University, I had my students come up with a song to remember the threats to internal and external validity. One day when they were taking an exam, I noticed heads bopping as if they were listening to music, and I realized they were using the song they'd made up to answer some of the test questions. Music is a powerful learning tool, and that is why it is also an excellent strategy for assessing learning of your content model.

If you are conjuring up memories of sleepless nights, sweaty palms, and test anxiety, stop! In the ENGAGE Model, assessments are not intimidating tests that make palms sweat from nerves. They are another opportunity for learners to enhance their confidence around the new learning and myelinate those paths to the new connections or skills. And this is a perfect time to celebrate.

Celebrating Brilliance and Assessing Learning

How many times have you learned something new, then walked out the door and promptly forgot it? Too many to count, right? It's typical. I remember getting taken to a spa for my birthday and learning in a seminar this seven-step wellness plan from a wonderfully talented teacher. I was fired up to reclaim my body's true strength by lifting weights and drinking veggie shakes. Unfortunately, once I got home and fell into my regular routine—family, work, and my daily four-mile walk—I couldn't remember the exact

CHAPTER 8 • STEP 5: GAUGE AND CELEBRATE

E	• Energize Learners
N	• Navigate Content
G	• Generate Meaning
A	• Apply to Real World
G	**• Gauge and Celebrate**
E	• Extend Learning to Action

seven steps of the plan. I never looked back, and I never integrated those seven steps into my life. Sustaining your commitment is tough.

This part of the ENGAGE Model is a quick, painless assessment that reveals to your hard-working learners just how much they have learned. The process of doing the assessments embeds the learning deeper in memory, which creates momentum for change. It's a celebration that sends learners out the door on a high note, aware and proud of how much they've learned. Your job is actually a lot of fun. You want to assess in a way that generates enthusiasm and motivation through an understanding of just how far they have come and how much they have learned. You also want to reinforce their sense of community, the bonds that they have developed. This is important for extending learning to real-life practice outside of the learning environment.

Before we dive into the many different testing or assessment strategies, let's draw a little insight from Bloom's taxonomy, a common educational questioning rubric that is not well known to people in fields outside of education. In 1956, Benjamin Bloom and a group of other psychologists created a classification system that divides educational objectives into three categories or domains: affective, psychomotor, and cognitive. Within this classification system, "learning at higher levels is dependent on having attained prerequisite knowledge and skills at lower levels."[1] The goal was to influence a more holistic approach to education. Bloom's taxonomy includes a system for the types of questions teachers could ask students. Through research, psychologists had found that over 95 percent of the questions asked of students were only at the lowest level, thus requiring very little mental effort.[2] The questions in Figure 8.1, which I created from Bloom's framework, apply to the simplest recall/recognition of facts or information to the most complex learning—evaluating what you have learned and defending it, predicting the future, and innovating from current knowledge. You might use it as a source to develop your assessment questions. You will have your participants celebrating even more!

Assessment Strategies

As you can see in the questioning rubric in Figure 8.1, you can use a wide variety of questions to challenge the learners to reflect and assess their learning. Those questions can be interwoven with the interactive strategies that I present here. Most are very elastic; you can modify them so they work for individuals or pairs, small groups or large ones. Let participants choose their assessment activities: they will enjoy the variety of strategies

Category from Simplest to Most Complex (Less to More Intellectual)	Verbs That Represent Categories	Questions You Could Ask to Use Higher Order Thinking (Work Their Brains)
Knowledge *(Facts, information, data, research)*	Arrange, label, list, name, recognize, recall, repeat, tell, write, locate, find	• Who, what, when, where? • What do you know about *X*? • What do you recall about *X*? • Matching test, timelines, list main concepts.
Comprehension *(Understanding, paraphrasing, summarize, retell)*	Describe, explain, identify, recognize, restate, translate, compare, interpret	• In your own words . . . • Outline the steps you would take to . . . • Build the following puzzle . . . • Can you select the correct answers from the list of options? • What was the main idea of *X*? • What are the differences between *X* and *Y*? • What is your definition of *X*?
Application *(Demonstrating facts, rules, and principles, showing ability to use—taking it from abstract to concrete)*	Apply, demonstrate, dramatize, solve, show, illustrate, construct, operate, practice, solve, use	• How would you show you could apply the concepts, techniques? • Illustrate the four different _____. • Role-play your new skills. • Use the new model to solve a real-world situation. • How would you teach someone to use this new information? • How is *X* an example of *Y*?
Analysis *(Arrangement, logic, difficulties, obstacles, wisdom)*	Subdivide, distinguish, examine, categorize, identify, separate, differentiate, calculate, experiment, question, test	• What obstacles may get in the way of you implementing *X*? • What is the benefit or value of applying *X*? • Why did *X* happen? • What are the consequences of *X*? • How does *X* compare/contrast with *Y*? • What evidence do you have for saying *X*? • Create a graph that shows the relationship between *X* and *Y*.

Figure 8.1. Questioning Rubric Based on Bloom's Taxonomy

Category from Simplest to Most Complex (Less to More Intellectual)	Verbs That Represent Categories	Questions You Could Ask to Use Higher Order Thinking (Work Their Brains)
Synthesis *(Creativity, innovation, imagination, new ideas, possibilities)*	Arrange, assemble, construct, create, invent, imagine, propose, devise, set up, formulate	• Write a case study that illustrates the concepts in a new setting. • If you could use any resources, what would you do to implement X? • What is a unique, original combination of ideas to do X? • What solutions could be combined to create a new option? • If you were king or queen of X, what would you do first?
Evaluation *(Feelings, emotions, intuition, gut instinct)*	Judge, appraise, argue, assess, defend, justify, recommend, assess, rate, predict	• How do you feel about X? • Create criteria to judge your performance on X (like a secret shopper). • What changes to X would you recommend? • How would you defend your position about X? • What do you think is best about X? Worst? • What criteria would you use to evaluate your desired outcome of X?

Figure 8.1. (Continued)

and will feel a strong sense of power and confidence, which will carry over into their actions.

I have started with the more unique ways to celebrate or assess learning and ended with more traditional ones such as multiple-choice tests. Remember—this step in the ENGAGE Model is your chance to inspire and connect the learners to the content, to each other, and to the results they are looking for from what they have learned to date.

3–2–1. The 3–2–1 strategy is a way of assessing learning that asks people at the end of a meeting or learning session to write the following:

3 key terms from what they've just learned

2 ideas they would like to learn more about

1 concept or skill they think they've mastered

Mind Mapping. Mind mapping is a good strategy for assessment. Invite those who want to use this method to one corner of the room, or have them stay at their tables. They will collaborate on a group mind map. You could have more than one group do mind maps, and they can use them to teach each other. If you are teaching virtually, you can do this in breakout rooms or private chats. Figure 8.2 is an example of a group mind map depicting all that they learned about retention of information.

Write a Song. Have the students write a song based on the theme of your model. For example, when I teach Legendary Customer Service, I say, "What song do you want people singing as they are walking away from you because you have delivered Legendary Customer Service and you are a legend in their minds?" Each table has to come up with a song. They usually come up with songs like "I Feel Good" and "We Are the Champions."

Another option is to have them create their own song, including the concepts and details, like my former physical science students did with the periodic table. If you are a gifted songwriter (musical intelligence), you can teach them a song with the concepts, and then everyone can sing to celebrate.

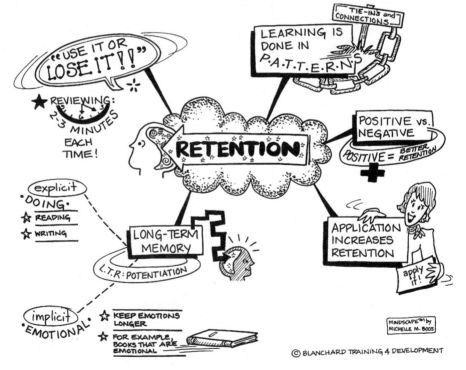

Figure 8.2. Mind Map on Learning and Retention

Stump the Panel. In this game, each learner writes five tough questions at their table and asks participants at the other tables to answer them. Their goal is to "stump the panel."

Make a Newsletter. Learners could create mock newsletters representing the big ideas and details of what they have just learned. For example, if I were teaching leadership, headlines for articles might be "Leaders Follow the Three Keys to Effective Leadership," "Retention Increases 50 Percent," or "Employee Work Passion Goes Up 20 Percent Due to New Leader Behaviors." Participants write brief articles to accompany their headlines. This is a great assessment tool for focusing on a main idea, and supporting concepts and details.

Share One Key Learning. In an assessment strategy for the entire group to do together, you facilitate by asking each participant to share one key learning. Everyone benefits by focusing on their key learning and by hearing the key learnings of others.

In face-to-face learning sessions, 90 percent of the time I end a class by zipping around the room and asking for one key learning they got from the session. This technique is a way of reviewing all the key learnings for the day, because the learners usually bring up all the important concepts on their own, which is the best way for learners to transfer their learning into their long-term memory. An extra benefit of this strategy is that participants often gain new perspective and see value in something by hearing another learner highlight something they didn't think was so important. This provides more aha moments and enables learners to see the value in all activities and concepts.

Create an Acronym. Use of acronyms as you navigate the content will enable key knowledge bits to be cemented in the brain. For example, "Roy G. Biv" equals red, orange, yellow, green, blue, indigo, violet, a mnemonic strategy for remembering the colors of the electromagnetic spectrum. If you were teaching managerial courage, you might have your learners make up an acronym for COURAGE. Have the learners write COURAGE vertically down the left side of a flip chart and then ask, "What attribute of courage does C stand for? What are the key takeaways of the day that link to that?" and so on until you complete the acronym. Once again, the energy it takes learners to create a mnemonic really challenges their brains and cements the learning.

Five Visible Signs. Ask learners to think, "What are the five visible signs of change other people will see in me as a result of today?" This strategy requires people to think about not just what they learned, but what they will *do* as a result of the learning.

Koosh Ball Review.   In a physical, fun quiz game, participants think of a couple of questions about the content of the session and then get into a wide circle or two lines. Someone throws a Koosh ball (or other small ball) to another participant and asks that person a question about the learning model. That person answers, then throws the ball to another and asks them a question, and around it goes. Be sure to give participants ample time to think of questions before the game.

Game Shows.   *Jeopardy* is a popular quiz game and a great assessment strategy. You or a designated student in a group give the answer. The contestants give the question. Other popular game shows can be adapted to work well, too. Also, there are numerous organizations that sell software to create customized games that use your questions and answers.

Crossword Puzzle Review.   There are a lot of Web sites you can subscribe to that will create a customized crossword puzzle for a nominal fee if you give them the questions or clues and the answers. People love these. Be sure you can solve your own crossword puzzle and that your clues and questions are clear. Sometimes a question that seems obvious can be confusing given other questions you may have asked.

Design a Model or Method.   Participants create their own model from what they have learned. In my capstone Executive MBA class at Grand Canyon University, students, individually or in teams, spend a few hours synthesizing all they have learned into a model for creating high-performing organizations. They then present their model to a panel of ex-students pretending to be with an organization that wants to hire them as consultants. It is a strenuous activity, but it is fun and amazingly integrative for the learners. It creates unique new connections to all of the previous learning from their coursework to date.

When I teach organizational change and review three or four change models, I have participants get into teams and create their own models. This is another comprehensive review of all the content taught, and it moves the learning to a new level of understanding and usefulness for the people in the class.

Multiple-Choice Test.   Remember when you were asked questions that had more than one answer and you filled in the bubble? The grass is (A) Green, (B) Purple, or (C) Magenta? Multiple choice is a good assessment option. Start with easier questions, and increase the level of difficulty as the test progresses.

CHAPTER 8 • STEP 5: GAUGE AND CELEBRATE

E	• Energize Learners
N	• Navigate Content
G	• Generate Meaning
A	• Apply to Real World
G	**• Gauge and Celebrate**
E	• Extend Learning to Action

Matching Test.   In this quick assessment, questions are on the left, and answers are on the right. Leave a line before the number so there is space to write A, B, or C.

____ 1. What is the color of the sky?　　(A) Orange
____ 2. What color is a tangerine?　　　(B) Green
____ 3. What color is grass?　　　　　(C) Blue

True/False Test.   A true/false test is an easy strategy for assessing knowledge and comprehension. Like the matching and the multiple-choice tests, it is best used in conjunction with other assessment strategies that are farther up Bloom's taxonomy, such as application, analysis, synthesis, or evaluation questions.

Short Answer Test.   A short answer test asks open-ended questions that have the learners process the knowledge, skills, and behaviors they have learned. For example, "What makes a goal SMART?" "What are the most important steps in listening effectively?" or "How will your use of the ENGAGE Model help your learners be brilliant?"

Build Confident Practitioners

The most important aspect of assessing and celebrating is creating learning experiences that send everyone out the door feeling brilliant—feeling a sense of wonder that makes them realize "Wow, I didn't even know this a few days ago (or an hour ago)," and "Hey, look how much I have learned." You want each learner thinking he or she is one of the smartest people that ever walked on the planet. Your goal was to create a learning session or multiple sessions that made it possible for individuals to learn and be smart, in the way that they learn best and *are* smart. This is when you see that you've accomplished that goal.

Although the assessments are lighthearted and more of a party, these activities add another layer of myelin to the axon to cement the learning deep within the brain so learners can access the knowledge when they leave your class. This is a very powerful byproduct of the participants realizing how much they have learned.

Dr. John Medina, author of *Brain Rules*, writes that repetition is the key to moving from short-term memory to long-term memory. "Repeat to remember and remember to repeat."[3] So include "repeat to remember" as part of the assessment strategy. Have the learners say aloud statements such as "I've done this," "I've learned that," and "I've overcome this." This repetition of key concepts as part of the assessment process helps to weave the pattern of actions into their world, and it will assist your learners in moving their new learning to long-term memory.

Another important byproduct of assessments is that they give your learners another opportunity to work with the entire model and all their accumulated learning. In other steps of the ENGAGE Model, learners usually worked with, assessed, and practiced with small chunks, but when they do the final assessment it is to evaluate their knowledge of the model as a whole and to apply it in their real world.

Picture Your Moment of Truth

Take a moment to envision what it will be like for you and your learners now that you have come this far and accomplished so much with them.

Gratitude and rewards abound!

Your students have worked hard, and so have you. You gave them the tools they needed to learn, to confirm their learning, and to compel them to want to teach others. You have celebrated their success with them and kept their energy and motivation high, while inspiring them to work harder and encouraging them to have fun while they are doing it. You have created a community of people who have bonded around learning your content. Working together, they harvested information, supported each other's success, and released more of those neurotransmitters that cement learning. Your learners are ready to walk out the door thinking and feeling "Wasn't that great? Wasn't that powerful?" They are fired up and eager to use their learning. And you know that you achieved your goal, the one you set when you said, "Here's my promise to you."

Celebration: You Are Brilliant!

Are you ready to celebrate? Take a moment to think about and appreciate how much you have learned about the Brilliance Learning System, the People, Content, and Learning Design (ENGAGE Model). Here are a few questions for your mini-celebration. I'll start out easy and move to a slightly higher level of difficulty.

1. What is the first G in the ENGAGE Model, and why is it important?
   a. G_____
   b. It is important because _____
      _____.

2. Who are the people in the equation? _____ and
   _____

3. The one who does the _____ is doing the learning.

4. It is not how smart people are, it is _____.

5. Using the first 70/30 Principle, when you are planning your learning experience, you should spend _____% of your time on *what* you are going to teach and _____% of your time on *how* you will teach it.

6. Your goal in having people practice, practice, practice is to increase m_____ and the neural connections.

7. Three ways to energize learners before they show up is to
   _____ or _____ or
   _____.

8. The concept of intense practice comes up often in this book. Why is practice so important to the achievement of your desired outcomes as you teach?

_____

_____

9. If you could only apply three key learnings and remember them for life, what would they be?

   a. _____

   b. _____

   c. _____

10. How will you set a target for yourself to be sure to follow up on your commitments to yourself and apply those three key learnings? Who will support you in your application? _____

_____

_____

_____

If the one who is doing the teaching is doing the learning, who will you teach this to _____ and by when _____?

11. Not done celebrating all you learned yet? Go ahead, celebrate some more by writing one last thought on something you want to remember as you seek to create *Brilliance by Design:*

_____

_____

_____

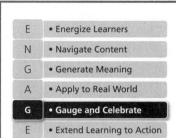

E	• Energize Learners
N	• Navigate Content
G	• Generate Meaning
A	• Apply to Real World
G	**• Gauge and Celebrate**
E	• Extend Learning to Action

Gauge and Celebrate

DO-IT-YOURSELF TEMPLATE

What will you do to have learners review and celebrate all they've learned while moving concepts from short-term memory to long-term memory?

What do you want to assess? _____

_____

_____

_____

_____

Which strategies would work best for you?

❏ Differentiate questions moving up Bloom's taxonomy.

❏ Create a group mind map.

❏ Play 3–2–1.

❏ Write a song.

❏ Stump the Panel (each learner makes 5 questions).

❏ Make a newsletter/newspaper headlines.

❏ Share one key learning.

❏ Create an acronym.

❏ Create 5 visible signs flip chart.

❏ Play Koosh ball review.

❏ Play *Jeopardy*/game show.

❏ Do crossword puzzle review.

❏ Design your own model from new information.

❏ Give multiple-choice test.

❏ Give matching test.

❏ Give true/false test.

❏ Give short answer test.

❏ Combination of the above.

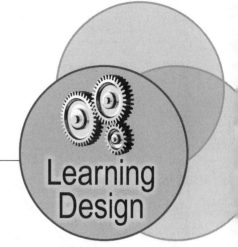

Learning
Design

CHAPTER **9**

Step 6: Extend Learning to Action

E	• Energize Learners
N	• Navigate Content
G	• Generate Meaning
A	• Apply to Real World
G	• Gauge and Celebrate
E	**• Extend Learning to Action**

I n a 2009 article for *Training and Development*, Fort Hill Company made the provocative statement "The finish line has moved"—suggesting that we're missing the boat if we think that a learning initiative stops when people walk out the door, hang up the phone, or leave their computer.[1] In Brilliance Learning System language, that means the goal is *moving brilliance to action*, or *getting the results*. Therefore, the final "E" in the ENGAGE Model is Extend Learning to Action to attain those results.

Help from a Friend

Before I joined Blanchard full time, I took their Situational Self Leadership class from their Learning Center. I loved it, I learned a lot, and I zipped back to my job of running the teaching and administrative credential programs at Chapman University in San Diego with every intention of putting my learning into practice so I'd be an effective self leader who acted on her game plan. One of the self-leadership activities was setting clear goals and sharing your most important goal with a learning accountability partner from the class. One of my goals was to write an article on the art of disciplining to build character for *Thrust for Educational Leadership,* the magazine for California school administrators. I felt that too often people were disciplining to give consequences for behavior rather than to teach. When I shared this intention with my partner in class, I was highly motivated to write that article. I gave myself a deadline of two months from the day I left the leadership class, and my accountability partner from class wrote that date down. Two months went by, and just like he said he would, my partner called me and said, "Hey, how are you doing on that article?" Yikes! His reminder of my goal was a rude awakening. I had thought about the article a couple of times, but I never wrote a word. Before we hung up, I promised to get started with it and let him know my progress by the following Friday. Within two weeks, I had written my article, "Disciplining for Character," and even shipped it off to the editor of the magazine. The editor liked it, said I had a "fresh, new voice," and asked me to write a monthly column, which I did for three years. (Be careful what you wish for!) We all know what it is to have excellent intentions but not always do what we have to do to move from commitment to action. It's amazing what happens when someone sets up a system of accountability to help you extend the learning into your day-to-day life.

There are some simple, excellent strategies to help learners, team members, or direct reports get support so that they move their commitments to action. You can connect at a profound level to support their commitments, catalyze their abilities, and ensure that they use their new knowledge.

Buddy Up

We all need assistance sometimes. That's one of the reasons assigning people a buddy before you leave the learning session or meeting is so powerful. You can weave this into the end of your assessment/celebration, or you can make it part of your closing. To begin with, you can ask everyone, "How many of you have ever worked with a coach or would like to do so? When they raise their hand, ask, "And what was the value or what would you expect the value to be of working with someone in this special relationship?" Many will probably say, "To help you do what you actually want to get done." When they say that out loud, pause and say, "Well, today is your lucky day. You won't get a professional coach, but you will get a professional buddy."

To begin this process, ask participants to stop and think of a clear goal. Then have them buddy up, share their goals, exchange contact information, and choose a date to be sure to call and ask their buddy questions, such as: What was your goal? How have you been doing with that goal? What would be the next step you want to take to act on that goal? When do you want to have that goal accomplished? What are the obstacles? What's getting in the way of your achieving your goal? What could you do about that? Review with your students the value of having this informal "coaching" relationship to help them act on their best intentions. Remind them to make a commitment each time they talk for the next follow-up to maintain a strong structure of continued accountability and mutual support.

E-Mail Reminders

You really want learners to use their new content within 24 to 48 hours. As you see in Figure 9.1 on recall and retention, timing is a critical factor. Since you want to help people use this learning fast, e-mail is a great tool. Send an e-mail within 24 hours asking them how they are doing and if they are acting on their best intentions. Give them a one-page worksheet to fill in and send back to you.

Share Success Stories

Additional e-mails you send can continue the power of the learning community by suggesting that participants share with you and each other how they have used the new content and gotten results. You can add an incentive.

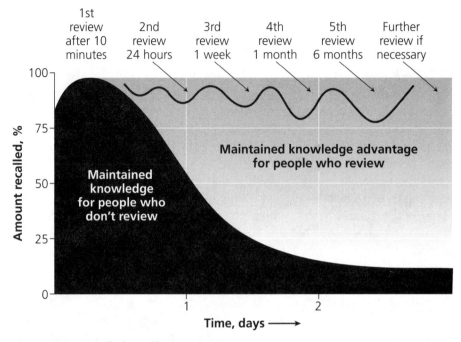

Figure 9.1. Recall Chart: The Learning Express
(Used with permission.)

When a learner announces or relates his or her success story thanks to recently learned skills and understanding, you can include the story in the next e-mail. These e-mails can also have links to many of the other suggestions included here.

Another strategy for obtaining success stories is to assign each participant a date their story is due to you. Let them know that you will be sending them a success story each week for 10 weeks or 50 weeks (the number equivalent to the number of people in the session). That way they have a commitment, and you have impactful stories to share each week to send along with other tips, summaries, and/or articles.

Link Learning to Business Outcomes

If possible, you want to link what people just learned to how it resolved a core business issue, and demonstrate this as a follow-up. Because you have been so clear from the beginning about the objectives you want people to achieve, as you extend the learning you'll want to share with people all the positive results and changes taking place. You may want to contact people via phone or e-mail, or perhaps you may want to connect with some people

E • Energize Learners
N • Navigate Content
G • Generate Meaning
A • Apply to Real World
G • Gauge and Celebrate
E • Extend Learning to Action

face to face to find out how they are applying their learning on the job. Ask clear, direct questions: "How have you been applying this learning?" "What has the value been of this learning to your business?" You could do an online survey using Zoomerang, Survey Monkey, or another simple survey generator. Or you could e-mail your own original survey with a few questions. You could add even more energy to the mix by getting together a small focus group, via conference call or in person, and asking them where the impact has been made on their business objectives. Ask them, "Where have you seen some return on investment from this training?" It is pivotal that you also report this back to the key sponsors—the people who would be interested in the application of what participants have just learned—and also that you create testimonials or posters with success stories and pictures.

Contests/Awards

Ask participants to let you know how they have used the information and shared it with other people. You might send a $5 gift card or another small gift to people for carrying the learning forward, teaching it to others, and impacting a behavior change.

Give another award to people who use the knowledge or skill the most. Let the group nominate each other for this award. If you just taught *The Hamster Revolution*[2] strategies to get control of e-mail, you may want participants to share examples of the best e-mails that people have written using the new A-B-C (Action–Background–Close) template to structure e-mails people want to read and respond to. You may create monthly awards with clever titles. This can be fun and energizing and can spark a spirit of novelty, driving eager anticipation for future learning.

Lunch and Learn

There are multiple ways to have Lunch and Learn review sessions. Think of these sessions as boosters. You could facilitate them face to face or virtually. While people eat their lunch, they can watch a video, read an article, or do another activity. Ask them to share where they have experienced success in applying their learning or where they are struggling. People can get into groups to brainstorm strategies. I had an eight-session, phone-only Lunch and Learn to follow up a two-day session on How to Maximize Learning for a large team of attorneys working for a biotechnology company. They all learned and talked about practicing two or three concepts a week. It was engaging and simple yet extremely valuable for these hardworking professionals who have to learn so much to be able to do their jobs well.

You may want to invite key sponsors to Lunch and Learn sessions. Ask learners to teach the sponsors what they have learned, practiced, and moved to action.

Provide Mentors

Previous participants are excellent mentors. You may want to choose a few stars to log into or physically be at the next class to share with participants how much they valued the learning and how they have put it to use. Utilizing these mentors to have small group discussions with people often helps them become champions of the content and may even increase their efficacy or self-esteem because they are sharing their brilliance. The synergy is powerful as people learn these new skills from someone who has been there in the trenches.

Podcasts

Podcasts are becoming an extremely popular way to reinforce learning and create deeper neural connections. A creative way to use this medium is to do interviews with people who have taken the class. Ask people to talk about how they have been using their new skill or knowledge. Ask them how the learning has made a difference—even small differences.

Consider using podcasts to review key concepts in your model or to talk about typical stumbling blocks. Give concrete examples and use stories that illustrate what you have been teaching. For example, if you were doing a podcast to reinforce the concept of rewards and recognition, you could tell an amazing story of someone you know who does an exemplary job of noticing and rewarding the good things people do. Then give other examples, and end with a challenge to listeners asking them to focus on what *they* think will be pivotal to their success. This might be as simple as deciding to ask their people, "If I were to reward you for a job well done, how would you like to be rewarded?"

Podcasts after sessions should help people apply what they're learning to their real world. In addition, you could send a podcast on a related subject. Maybe you have a friend or a peer who has key content that would be of interest.

E-Freshers

E-freshers are 30-minute sessions in the virtual classroom where people come together to drill down on key concept areas and celebrate progress that has been made, while discussing new commitments they would like to

E	• Energize Learners
N	• Navigate Content
G	• Generate Meaning
A	• Apply to Real World
G	• Gauge and Celebrate
E	• Extend Learning to Action

make. You pick a subtopic you want to dive deeper into and offer examples, clear stories that illustrate key concepts, and interactive exercises that get the participants—maybe even team members—practicing. Always end an e-fresher with people sharing their key learnings in the chat box or on the phone to reinforce concepts.

Team Support Groups

At sessions that involve teams of people, each team can also be its own support network, and each one usually will have a designated leader. If you have established this framework, you can keep in touch with those leaders and help them to share great content with their group. Help them have the language and practice to support and move their learning to action.

Letters

Handwritten letters are underused, even though they are an incredibly powerful strategy for extending learning. Write a note to each learner thanking him or her for participating in the session with you and for bringing the best of who they are to the occasion. If you had them write a letter to themselves with their commitment as part of your session, this would be a good time to send it back to them. To set this up: In class, have participants write a letter to themselves with their intentions so that you can mail it two weeks to a month after the session to remind them of the commitments they made to themselves. In addition, you could send an article, a template, or some other key information that would help them.

Leverage Managerial Support

If you are training in a corporate setting, to sustain learning you may want to have a session where you meet with the managers of the people who were at the session. Share with them what people learned and the impact on them, what general commitments were made, and how management can leverage the learning by having a conversation where their people teach them what they learned. Remind participants that you will do this and that you will keep all personal insights confidential.

Coaching

Recommend that people find and work with a coach, someone who has been trained to lobby for learners in applying their skills and techniques. A coach is invested in their success. A study by Jack Zenger, Joe Folkman, and

Robert Sherwin makes a strong case for the significant impact on productivity and results when you follow up a learning event with coaching to support you in attaining your goals.[3] Coaches set clear agreements and outcomes and use a wide array of high-impact strategies to enable people to act on their intentions—to move learning to action.

When I took a time management class, I was fired up and extremely motivated to redo my schedule and become more efficient with my time in calendaring. However, due to the large number of things I needed to get done, I found that I wasn't using the new skills I had learned in the class. It wasn't until I worked with a coach around my stress over having too much to do that I realized my issue was not actually a tactical time management problem. It was my belief about being busy that kept me feeling overwhelmed. My belief was born out of one of my first jobs, which was at a large department store where I stocked packages of disposable diapers and other baby goods. As fast as I stocked those huge boxes of diapers, they sold. In that job, if I tried to take my break, my boss harassed me; in fact, he didn't seem to actually do anything but harass employees. As long as I was busy doing something, everything was perfect, but when I tried to take my 10-minute break or have my lunch he would reprimand me and make me feel negligent. The belief I unconsciously adopted because of the incessant harassment from my boss was, "Being busy is safe, and relaxation leaves you vulnerable to attack." My coach helped me realize that my stress and struggle to have extra time in my life was not a time management issue (no time to get it all done) but an underlying belief issue that I had to keep working all the time to feel safe.

It took quite a few sessions of working with the coach, including follow-ups, for me to incorporate a new behavior based on a different belief—because as I would schedule downtime I would get anxious. The coach had me sit with and embrace that anxiety, and realize that building the new habits I wanted for my life would take time. The time management problem took care of itself as I started scheduling breaks, and my brilliant coach helped me achieve the goal I had when I first took the time management class, which was to have more time for myself and my family.

Parties/Games/Fun

One final idea to extend learning is to just bring people together to reconnect. Go to a baseball game, have a party or a picnic, and take pleasure in the camaraderie and joy of being friends who learned together.

E • Energize Learners
N • Navigate Content
G • Generate Meaning
A • Apply to Real World
G • Gauge and Celebrate
E • Extend Learning to Action

Extend learning to other places.

REFLECTION: Exercise

EXTEND LEARNING

- How will you extend your learning so you have a greater transfer from learning to achieving business results through application of new skills?

- What other great ideas keep learning alive for you?

E	• Energize Learners
N	• Navigate Content
G	• Generate Meaning
A	• Apply to Real World
G	• Gauge and Celebrate
E	• **Extend Learning to Action**

Extend Learning to Action
DO-IT-YOURSELF TEMPLATE

What else would extend the learning and help people act on their best intentions?

❏ E-mail reminders

❏ Coaching

❏ Success case studies/stories

❏ Business impact contest—dollarize—show results in action

❏ Giving each person a buddy

❏ Getting manager involved

❏ Letter to self—mailing a letter they wrote themselves with their intentions

❏ Awards contests for best use

❏ Podcast follow-ups

❏ E-freshers in virtual classrooms

❏ User teams

❏ Mentor from a previous class

❏ Job aids as a reminder

❏ Phone review sessions

❏ Posters with key model, strategies

❏ "Tip of the Week"

❏ Lunch and Learns

❏ Video contest

❏ Interviews with stars in newsletter

❏ Peer nominations for awards

❏ Individual coaches

❏ Team support group

CHAPTER **10**

Bringing Out Brilliance
in the Virtual Classroom

The principles that underlie teaching or training live in the virtual classroom are much the same as teaching or training in a physical classroom. Your goal is to connect people, at a deep level, to information and strategies that have the ability to transform their world. Learners often don't have the same previous experience with virtual learning as they do with classroom learning. It might be new to them, or they may have had a negative experience with it. This is why aligning your intentions with learning design is so important. What does this mean? It means you need to structure learning in a virtual situation so that it is clear—even clearer than in a physical classroom—and more nurturing. Create a human connection, despite physical distance, and use the technology as an asset. You have to make your point quicker, use shorter introductions to content, and keep your learners' attention through interactivity.

This chapter addresses the special considerations inherent in learning and teaching in the virtual environment. For a complete understanding of the Brilliance Learning System and the ENGAGE Model, read the introduction and Chapters 1 through 9. These chapters contain an abundance of

Virtual learning is fun!

information to help support you in the virtual classroom and to bring out brilliance in your learners.

There are two approaches to virtual facilitation in this chapter. Part I is a general or overarching understanding of the concepts underlying effective live synchronous virtual training. Part II describes the virtual learning experience through the lens of the ENGAGE Model, from signing on with learners to closing the session so you can bring out the brilliance in the virtual classroom.

Traditional Classroom versus Virtual Classroom

Training in the virtual classroom enables learning to come alive for people in geographically dispersed locations. It can be fun, rewarding, and intricate.

Before we begin, what do you see as the difference between traditional face-to-face learning and real-time virtual learning? Figure 10.1 explains some of my own thoughts on these differences.

Differences in Learning Methods	
Traditional	**Virtual**
You can see the students.	You must picture your audience.
You see students thinking.	You hear silence.
You ask a question, and one person answers.	You ask a question on white board or chat box, and everyone answers.
You can talk for 5 to 7 minutes without losing the attention of the students.	Every 2 to 3 minutes, you need some type of interaction to hold interest.
You can use tests to see if students are learning.	With polls, quizzes, practices, or chat, you get instant, anonymous feedback to know if students are learning.
You're a facilitator.	You're a radio talk show host: content must engage, and you must emote.
If people lose interest, they stay in class and multitask.	You can't see when people lose interest; they minimize you on their computer screens, and *poof!* they're gone.
Introverted people are more comfortable speaking up in small groups at their tables.	Introverted people are often shy and reluctant to speak up as the only voice.
You use body language, facial expression, and your voice to communicate.	You must use • An active listening voice. • Inflection to convey intentions and feelings. • Skill to anticipate ideas. • Clarity in asking questions. • Summary thoughts.
There is feedback at the end.	You have constant feedback loops for checking in.

Figure 10.1. Differences between Traditional Learning and Virtual Learning

Part I: Virtual Training Concepts

This section is about helping you feel more comfortable facilitating in a situation where you can't see your audience though you have the desire to positively impact every person present, just as you do in a physical or live face-to-face class or meeting. As you see depicted in Figure 10.2, successful virtual training involves the following interrelated concepts:

- Learner care
- Interactivity
- Fun
- Engaged emotions
- Technological tactics
- Learner-centered content and process
- Abundance of new insights
- Connection to the culture
- Walking the talk
- Listening up
- A Wondrous Workbook

Your awareness of these concepts can help you keep your learners attentive and committed (which is no easy feat given the abundance of competing, exciting content in their e-mail folder or on the Web). Part I of this chapter focuses on these concepts. You will notice the similarities to the concepts and strategies in Chapters 4 through 9, and you will want to use a lot of those ideas as well. This chapter, however, spotlights key distinctions for how to ENGAGE in the virtual world where learners may have greater trepidation and may arrive with many negative experiences of being held accountable for content taught poorly in previous virtual sessions.

Take Care of Learners

Learner care means that, regardless of your virtual platform, you make the participants who are meeting with you virtually feel nurtured even before they arrive by anticipating what they need to help them feel comfortable and smart and to help them succeed. Caring in this sense means giving extremely clear directions about how to log on, what materials they have to bring, why the session is needed, and why it's relevant to them, as well as other information to generate interest such as why other learners have thought it was so valuable.

To help learners know what to do, how to do it, and when to show up, you need to start with a thoughtful, conscious plan. Remember, it often takes more focused energy from learners to first get started with a virtual

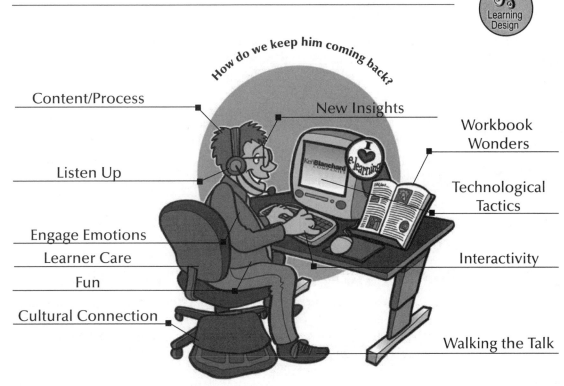

Figure 10.2. Vital Concepts of Virtual Training

learning session than it does for them to physically walk into a class. In your plan, you need to consider marketing the benefits and having multiple touch points. From the first e-mail on, you need to establish a caring environment where learners feel supported as they take on the task of learning unfamiliar platforms. To excite and focus them, you might want to send a learning packet ahead of time with the pre-work, participant workbook, some kind of edible treat, and perhaps a little rubber ball (you can get 36 tiny "porcupine balls" for about $6.00 online at orientaltradingcompany .com), a sign for their office door that says "Virtual Learning in Process," or other information about the class.

There should be a sense from this preexposure to the class that there is passion for the upcoming learning, and that the overall goal is their success. You may want to e-mail them a podcast or audio file with a welcoming introduction from the sponsor of the program or an overview of coming attractions (think movie trailer). In addition, the learner care needs to allow learners to feel assured that someone's going to be there to anticipate their every need and help them thrive in the virtual classroom. Learner care, done well, has people saying, "Wow! Who knew virtual learning was going to be this cool?" A couple of key points to remember about learner care:

- Make everything simple, clear, and easy. *Be sure you know their technological readiness.*

- Give them a number to call or an e-mail address to connect them with someone if they need help getting their computer ready, loading any software, or accessing the virtual platform. You want them showing up confident, happy, and ready to go versus cranky or annoyed because the technology didn't work.

Keep a Learner-Centered Focus

Keeping a learner-centered focus helps you achieve your mutual objectives. Think about what you want learners to be able to do at the end of the session. If you keep the end in mind, you will get there. You want to make the most of your time, balancing hard work and practice with fun, connection, motivation, and meaning. Everything you do to keep the learning session focused on the learners supports them and helps them to experience the content in a meaningful way so they can teach each other, practice, and apply.

Your first goal is to celebrate your learners for who they are and the expertise they bring, and to thank them for participating in this event. By asking questions immediately, before the session even starts, and encouraging active participation, you are showing the learners the session is all about them. They realize that their involvement is crucial. I often start a virtual training session by asking people where they are calling in from and what's new in their world. If anything newsworthy has been happening, I ask about it. Or I might ask them what movies they have seen recently—anything to get them talking right from the beginning so they know *this class is about them, for them, and involving them.*

Next, I share the *journey map.* Unlike learners in the face-to-face classroom where they walk in, sit down, and can predict what's going to happen, learners in a virtual classroom often are not aware of what to expect or how the session will flow. They hear or see that there are four sessions, but they may wonder what that means. They may wonder whether they are supposed to work in between sessions, and if so, how much. A journey map helps to show all of this visually as it walks them through the full course so they have clarity, confidence, and a feeling of anticipation of what's to come. Because they see where they are going, they get excited at the prospect of reaching that goal. It's like traveling by car and seeing on the map that Cincinnati is 60 miles away. You see the landmarks on the map between you and Cincinnati and feel comfortable that even though you've never been there before, you can confidently move forward down the road, knowing what's ahead of you. Throughout your trip, you see Cincinnati getting closer and closer: now it's only 40 miles away, now it's 20 . . . The anticipation of reaching the destination generates energy. It's the same with virtual learning. You create anticipation by showing the destination and landmarks to inspire learners to push forward through the trip.

Learner-centered content ensures that the content really relates to the learners specifically—to their career and to their life. In the physical classroom, you begin with out-of-context practice and then move it to in-context practice. You do the same in the virtual environment. You also start with easy, low-risk questions and build to more rigorous interactive exercises to create a safe environment for learners, help them build confidence, and ensure success. Be sure to create an atmosphere where people can be right. One of my earliest mistakes was to call on people who hadn't volunteered early on when it was a little too high-risk, and then I would never hear from them again throughout the session. Poof! They would just disappear.

Lastly, you will want to utilize a variety of accelerated learning practices and adapt to different learning styles, acknowledging that visual, auditory, and kinesthetic learners all take in information and learn differently. You want to make sure that kinesthetic learners are clicking on the screen, typing in the chat box, or writing in their workbooks or on a piece of paper. For auditory learners, you want to ask questions so the learners are subliminally thinking of the answers, getting in touch, and talking with each other. Allow them to speak on the phone every now and then. Multiple voices stimulate the brain. Have images, graphs, and pictures, not just text, in your slide deck to speak to the visual learner. It also really helps virtual learners if you have the luxury to engage with them by separating them into breakout rooms and letting them talk and process their thoughts, just as they would if they were in a live classroom. In their breakout rooms, they can also create whiteboards where they are drawing and brainstorming with their peers. This builds community and deepens neurological connections to the new practices you are teaching. (See Chapter 5 for more on learning styles and recommended activities.)

Drive Success with Interactivity

I often start virtual sessions by asking people to type their responses in the chat box to the question "What do you need in order to be able to learn?" Interactivity is often at the top of their list. As discussed in the previous section, you want to vary strategies, keep them interactive, and appeal to kinesthetic, auditory, and also visual learners. Ask participants to raise their hand if they agree with someone's comment, or give you a red check or a green X as a response. Have them raise their hand if they would like to ask a question. Interactivity every two to three minutes sustains focus and keeps learners on their toes. Conduct a poll. Encourage them to chat, draw, and ask questions, and have them write down their answer, annotate, or put a check on the screen. Other strategies for interactivity include having learners write in the workbook, participate in a breakout session, or do an activity where they practice with a partner by writing their thoughts to different questions and go back and forth sharing in a private chat. Keep reengaging and refocusing them at a level that keeps them actively involved. If you talk too long in the virtual classroom, learners will get distracted and want to look at their e-mail, check their voicemail, or make shopping lists, and they will minimize you on their computer screen.

Trigger New Insights

Just like a great radio talk show, the virtual classroom needs to have bright ideas, new insights, and maybe a big aha every five to seven minutes. These new insights might be generated from taking polls that ask the really tough questions, such as "If customer service is so easy, why aren't people doing it?" "Why aren't there more best bosses?" "What makes a challenging conversation so challenging?" "Think of someone you really trust—not someone you like, but someone you trust. What makes you trust this person?" The answers to these questions can lead to insights that are both professional and personal. It reminds them to use what they are learning in their personal lives to stimulate a love of sharing learning.

Have Fun

The virtual classroom should be fun. Bring your best sense of humor. Participants should want to be there because they're having a good time: the learning is important to them, and at the same time it is entertaining and engaging in the moment. Fun strategies include unique activities like having participants play review games such as *Jeopardy,* doing Q&As, matching questions 1–5 with answers A–E, or having cartoons or funny pictures in your slide decks.

Share with them why they got a toy porcupine ball in their materials. Tell them you know that many of them might be kinesthetic learners and need something to fiddle with while they are learning. Other fun ideas include playing games like "Stump Your Neighbor," where they type questions in the chat box for other people to try to answer. You can promise fabulous virtual prizes, like a picture of candy or a new car (just to be silly). Or you could put their name into a drawing for a prize like a gift card, which they would receive in the mail after the session. Playing a review game with questions that have four possible answers called "Who Wants to Be a Bizillionaire?" with the music from *Who Wants to Be a Millionaire* is engaging. Music is also a great tool that adds novelty in the virtual classroom. Fun TV or movie theme songs make people smile. Something like the theme from *Mission: Impossible* releases a little tension when doing a tough case study and creates a sense of joy in learning.

Another thing you can do is go to YouTube and find short videos to play that are heart-moving. An example might be to show the video of contestant Paul Potts on *Britain's Got Talent* and ask leaders, "Who has a singer like this getting by as a cell phone salesperson?" Show examples of things you are teaching. To extend learning, provide concrete examples that will pique learners' interest.

I like to play *Name That Tune*. One of my favorite things is to watch people who have absolutely no desire to play a game like *Name That Tune* come up with a song that a customer might be singing when walking away from them if they have had great service, like James Brown's "I Got You (I Feel Good)." I always start this activity by asking people to give me a green check if they woke up today wanting to play *Name That Tune*. They laugh, I get a few checks, and we're off to have fun.

Make a Cultural Connection

Another principle of virtual learning is to create a community that thrives in the particular culture in which you're working. A way you might do this is to have a senior leader in the company share his or her commitment to this initiative right at the beginning of your training. Maybe have a video or an audio clip with a picture of them on the slide. Ask the senior leader to prerecord why it is so important that the participants learn what they are about to learn, why they should be involved, and what the organizational imperative is that relates to this new learning. Flip videos and other technology make it very easy to have someone do a little three- to five-minute video, greeting the learners and linking their learning to an important purpose in their job and the mission of the company. They might say, "I'm so excited that you are taking this training. Our company needs you and your best thoughts so much as we move to . . ." This says to participants, "I care about you, and we really value you and what you're about to learn." It also says they are the organization: "Without you, we would not get results or create an organization where people can do their best work."

Another way to connect to their culture is to keep weaving the brilliance from people's responses into the fabric of the session. So if Lisa said she has been doing mini-comparison demonstrations that have significantly increased her sales of the new very-difficult-to-sell handwash, and later on Bill says he is really struggling to meet his numbers on the same product because it's so much more expensive than the competition, that's where you would connect Bill with Lisa and ask if they would be willing to work together. You might say, "Lisa, would you be willing to chat with Bill privately so he can get your contact information to learn how you do that?" This way, you are building a community of learners who are all working to help the entire organization improve performance while creating a culture of learners and teachers.

> Build a community of learners who are all working to help the entire organization improve performance while creating a culture of learners and teachers.

Using client- or department-specific case studies and content is another way to link to the culture. People hear their own voice and see their own world in the scenarios, which enables them to feel that you know them and their needs, and that the situations you are putting them in are setting them up for success in their world.

Woven throughout your presentation could also be testimonials from prior participants. These could be written quotes on your slide deck that you don't actually mention, or they could be put into the workbook as side notes. The message you are telling participants is, "People just like you in your organization value this learning."

Lastly, your goal in any learning situation is to help the organization get the key business results they are looking for. Throughout your session, you should make explicit links to the exact goals of the organization. In addition, if you do pre-work or any assignments, have participants interview each other about very specific situations that are currently going on in the organization. As part of your preparation for this learning event, it is important that you do some research, find out ahead of time what is going on in the company, and understand the experience of the participants so that the content really resonates with their culture, issues, and current needs and desires.

Engage Emotions

The emotional connection you have with your learners is another one of your secrets to success in the virtual classroom. You need to become comfortable addressing and acknowledging people's feelings—the full range of their emotions. You may want to read up on the subject of emotional intelligence, which is about being aware of and managing your own emotions as well as the emotions of others.[1] Your knowledge of this subject may help you get people immersed in discussion of tough questions, and it also may give you insight into why there is sometimes a lack of responsiveness.

Think about why people listen to talk radio. The controversial topics discussed in the programs trigger emotional responses that engage and acknowledge how listeners are feeling. Leverage and acknowledge emotional messages throughout your content. You also can motivate and tap into the emotions of learners by consistently, every 10 minutes or so, asking questions such as "What's in it for you to be learning this?" "What's in it for you to listen at a deeper level? How will that help you? Why is that important to you?" "What's in it for you to learn to be more present with people when you're coaching them?" Subliminally as you teach, your goal is to figure out who your participants want to be and to help them, through this learning, grow into the person they are trying to be.

> Subliminally as you teach, your goal is to figure out who your participants want to be and to help them, through this learning, grow into the person they are trying to be.

You also want to engage emotions by celebrating learning and using music and success stories. If there is more than one session, when they come for the second part have them celebrate the success they had with their previous learning. Learning something new and actually using it elicits a powerful emotion. Strong emotions have the ability to create lasting memories that can drive future behavior. Since there's a powerful need to be present and engage the emotions of all learners, it is optimal to keep your class sizes between 12 and 20, and sessions at 90 minutes followed by a 30-minute break, to enable you to really listen and touch (virtually) all participants.

Walk the Talk

Walking the talk means that you are enabling people to use the material as fast as possible. In the virtual classroom, people want to see progress right away. They want to hear you bring up the issues draining their time and energy, along with innovative solutions. Remember, they're on their own. They're staring at their computer. They need frequent reminders that what they are learning is changing their life, right then, right in every moment.

It is even more important that you have tools—job aids, conversation starters—any materials that enable them to instantly apply their knowledge. The virtual classroom must be a supportive place where, as they try these new skills with peers and experts, they feel safe to experiment. Consistently share your gratitude for the fact that they are taking a risk to put it out there and try something new that may be difficult. It's important as you kick off your session that you start right off by sharing with participants that they are going to be actively involved, that they are going to be participating, and that the only way to really learn is to speak up and try something new. Your goal is to help them walk the walk. You want them, before they leave the virtual classroom, to have had a chance to practice what it is that you're preaching so that they want to run and apply it and teach other people. Think viral marketing!

One last way to help people walk the walk virtually is by allowing virtual learners to partner up and coach each other in between sessions. Connecting them to a peer who is going to call them or talk to them will help them overcome obstacles, identify areas to come back and talk about, and build on the experience they've had with you.

Use Technological Tactics

Technology is a glorious place to build a community. Unlike physical classrooms where participants raise hands and answer questions one at a time, in the virtual classroom your 12 to 20 participants all answer the question at the same time. It's a fascinating slice of what everyone's thinking. Leverage this new technology all you can to take advantage of the innovative learning methods it offers. Strategies for doing this include using polls. For example, if you hear people having a discussion, you can instantly say, "Let's see who else thinks this way. Let's take a poll—how many of you would say you strongly believe in this plan of action we are about to take? How many feel like it needs more work?" Get an instant pulse on the group.

Another way to use technology is creating beautiful graphics that shift the mind and graphically depict concepts that aren't as impactful in words alone. Instead of saying, "55%, 35%, 10%," make a pie chart with those numbers. This instantly gives a visual snapshot to show the depth and distinctions between the numbers. Images often are more powerful and create a stronger memory.

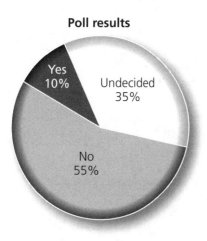

Figure 10.3.
Example of Poll Results Pie Chart

Compare the pie chart in Figure 10.3 with a line of text simply stating, "55% No, 10% Yes, 35% Undecided." Which has greater meaning?

Other technological tactics would include creating an Internet site where people can gather as a community of learners, writing a blog where people can respond, or creating a wiki where people can write about what they have done to move their learning to action, ask questions, or post experiences they have had. You might try including flash animation so that people can drag and drop right there on the screen or click on a link and go to a video on another site. Using all the technology available to you deepens the learning through multisensory approaches.

Listen Up

"Listening up" is of utmost importance in any learning situation. You need to be more mindful of it when doing virtual training. "Listening up" means you are picking up on what's *not* being said and bringing it out. Like a coach, you challenge the ease with which people say "yes" or "no," and prod them to go deeper, expanding their thinking. This helps intensify their desire to listen to the conversation, because it's so interesting. For example, if someone says, "My best boss appreciated me." Instead of saying, "Oh! That's great. We all love to be appreciated," a coach might say, "Tell me more about that appreciation. What did that boss actually do to make you feel appreciated? How did that make you feel? What did you learn from that best boss about the power of appreciation?" Allow people time to speak—and then really *listen* to the subtleties of what is said. Multiple voices enable the brain to shift, refocus, and feel more enlivened.

To use *listening up* as an activity, try "brown bag" phone calls. These are follow-up learning sessions in which you facilitate a 20-minute phone call touching on one of the key concepts you wanted to elaborate on. Everyone on the call brings their lunch and participates in the follow-up. You might create four sessions that cover four different points—but be sure to allow half the time to talk about the point and the other half to help people celebrate what they have learned or ask questions. Once again, your goal is to listen to where they are and what they need to really continue processing and learning at the deepest level. As Scott Blanchard, motivational speaker and trainer, says, you should "listen with the intent of being influenced." With the subconscious mind working 80,000 times faster than the conscious mind, people can sense if you really mean what you say and if you are interested in their growth and development and processing of what you are talking about.[2]

Resist Repeating Yourself

It is a common practice for people who train virtually to repeat themselves because they don't actually see people nodding when they are talking. Control the urge to do this. One strategy to help is to put up a picture of people where you can see it so that as you speak you can see images of faces in your mind.

Provide a Wondrous Workbook

Your workbook represents you and your unique style as an instructor. Learners will find it more appealing if it is clever and incorporates images, quotes, and plenty of space for participants to write. Craft your content so that it will really help them answer questions in the chat box, interact, and then have something to go back to for reference.

Pick and choose your workbook content carefully. Try to create something that flows, with images and quotes, cartoons, drawings, and space to doodle or take notes. You want your workbook to respond to the brain's need for novelty. This keeps the participants engaged while they are by themselves trying to learn in this community. Include job aids in your workbook (see Chapter 2 for more on job aids) as well as other tools to help people be successful. It's also a good idea to designate space for participants to write their ideas, insights, and intentions. Content that only requires learners to click on the screen or barely respond doesn't require a workbook page. For example, if you are asking an important but rhetorical question and you're just getting a feel for what they think, you don't need a workbook page for that.

Part I Review: Keys to Success in the Virtual Classroom

You can maximize your learners' interest, alertness, and involvement throughout your meeting or training session with these tips and strategies.

1. Engage emotions. Ask tough questions so people want to listen.

2. Listen to their voices, not just your own.

3. Get to the point quickly so people don't minimize you on their computer screen.

4. If you want learners to do an activity where they need to write or design something, do the work yourself so that you know how long it takes and you won't have to keep asking, "Are you done?" Ask people to give you a green check to let you know when they are finished so you know everyone has completed the activity.

5. Be comfortable with silence. Just as if you're face to face with people, there are times when people have their heads down and are working diligently. You want to be comfortable with silence so that it gives them a chance to do their best work.

6. Use funny pictures and even more visuals than usual.

7. Use humor—a lot of it—to make people laugh.

8. Play music or use sound effects to go with pictures and games.

9. Use images that depict concepts and stimulate dialogue. For example, if you're teaching how to work with your people to create action plans, you may want to put up a picture of two icebergs with the captions "Leader" and "Direct Report," and ask why it's so difficult to work with and develop people. That image sparks a very different kind of conversation around how we often show little of who we really are and how the part that is below the surface might take a deep dive to see.

10. Have participants rate themselves on different polls to see if they are getting the concept.

11. Keep the pace quick and dynamic.

12. Listen to responses, and ask for more. Say, "Tell me more." Ask, "What can you do to prevent that?" "How did you do that?" Probe people's responses. Say things like "Very perceptive of you" and "Could you say more about that?"

13. Don't repeat your concepts, but tie them back to other comments participants have made about previous concepts or examples.

14. Be specific and descriptive. Instead of saying, "Good," "Great," or "Interesting," think about what you really like about what someone has said and tell them. Is it informative? Perceptive?

15. Use multiple learning styles to explain the most important constructs. You might have participants listen to an audio file or watch a short video. You might include in the workbook a script exemplifying a conversation. You could ask two participants to volunteer to read it or act it out. Then you break it down and have people share what they just heard.

16. Have them make up songs, draw pictures, or practice a conversation with another person in the chat box.

17. Involve people in building diagrams, charts, or pictures right on the screen. They can type on a whiteboard or write on a PowerPoint that has been started.

18. Use mini-assessments throughout the presentation. "You just learned X—let's show you how well you know it."

19. Reference research on occasion, such as studies that were conducted on the topic, to ratchet up buy-in from participants.

Part II: ENGAGE in the Virtual Classroom

This section walks you through the ENGAGE Model so you can design and deliver virtual training that brings out the brilliance in people. It is filled with concrete ideas for creating an environment where learners thrive and engage with their hearts and minds. Facilitating virtually, as you've read, has a new set of variables. You don't have the advantage of physically seeing your learners, so you don't have the visual cues that let you know whether they are really learning or you've lost them. You need to create activities that inspire, connect, and engage right from the beginning.

Energize Learners

Learners need to feel excited about your class. You want every contact you have with them—the e-mails you send, the workbook, and the images they see when they sign on to the class—to support a growing sense of excitement and anticipation that this course is something they need. Make sure your e-mail is welcoming and really articulates the reason they are taking the class. Point out benefits to them to help them delight in the fact that they are about to show up to something interesting.

Care for Yourself, and Check Your Technology. Take the time to care for yourself so you can be at your best and care for your learners. Give yourself an hour before the session starts and everyone signs on to get in the zone of being a good listener, settling into who you are and what your goal is for being together with your learners. Think of the three or four things participants will be able to do differently as a result of being in your session. Your ability to sustain your own energy sets the tone for others to be energized.

Be sure to breathe, drink water, and stand up to increase energy. If you tend to be someone who is very calm and talks slowly, you may want to bring your level of energy up a bit before you start. If you are high energy and you tend to speak fairly rapidly, you may want to do something to calm down. (I take a couple of deep breaths and drink a glass of milk!)

During this time, it's important to make sure the platform is working, the phone lines are up and ready to go, and you can sign on easily, move your slides, and make transitions. It's a good idea to turn on a backup computer in case yours crashes.

Focus Learners and Get to Know Them. Participants usually sign on five to seven minutes early. This is a great opportunity to get to know each of them personally. Ask them what's going on in their world just as if they were on the phone with you alone. Introduce yourself—say hello to every single person, individually, as they sign in. Put a map on the screen and ask them where they are calling in from, and how the weather is, or ask what's new in their world. You could prepare a slide that says, "Share in the chat box the funniest job you have ever had or an interesting fact about yourself." Ask them what books they are reading. Give them something to do

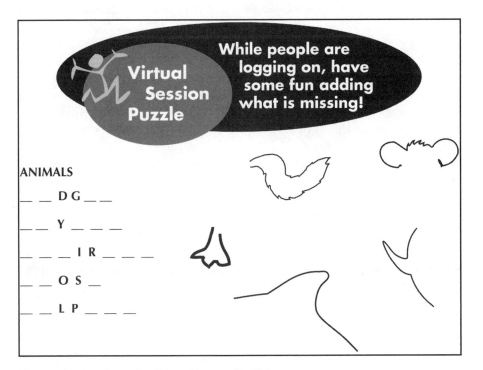

Figure 10.4. Example of Virtual Interactive Slide

that makes them realize that from the second they sign in, they are an integral part of this community. *Creating a first impression that communicates how important they are can make or break the session!*

You might have a puzzle on the screen for people to solve as soon as they sign on. It gives them something fun to play with. It can be squiggles that they have to complete, or country names with missing letters to fill in, or key content areas that you're going to teach. Make sure you explain where you want people to type information for these warm-up activities, on the screen or in the chat box. You want to be sure everyone knows how to use the interactivity tools.

Navigate Content

Presenting your new content in the virtual classroom begins with a road map that shows participants, step by step, what they're going to experience and how this new content is going to be presented to them. It begins with an energizing question that has them sit up and see the power in learning this material. Ask your first powerful question, which will focus the learners on your most important concept. As they type their thoughts, explain to them that this is the core of what they are going to be learning.

Start Strong. After you have gone over the agenda and shared the road map, you want to discuss what materials will be used and give participants an emergency phone number if anything happens to their connection. Let them know up front that you'll be randomly asking them for their comments throughout this process because you want to make it clear that active participation by them enhances learning. I always tell them that the one who is doing the talking is doing the learning, and I want them to learn as much as possible so I will be calling on them.

As you present content, explicitly state where you are in the flow of the road map. Participants will appreciate your guidance in helping them hone in on where you are and where you're going to be going.

Present Content in Digestible Pieces and Build. Present new content in small bites. Start with easier concepts, review as you go along, and build to more complex concepts and more robust activities that will be higher risk. You want learners interacting with the content, with each other, and with you every two to three minutes. What does this mean for you? You will give a small bit of information, then facilitate some kind of chat, discussion, poll, or quiz that helps them drill down on what they just learned.

Create a Safe Environment.   For many, responding virtually may be a bit threatening at first. You can minimize their anxiety by making sure the first few questions you ask are the type that are answered anonymously. Participants respond by checking off an answer on the screen.

You can also help people feel safe and less anxious by having them use the chat box to respond to questions or practice a skill. This is a good tool for responding to questions that require deep knowledge or prior knowledge, perhaps from having done a pre-work assignment. Also, only call on people once you see that they have completed their response in the chat box. This creates a safe environment.

Expand Thinking.   As participants type in the chat box, you want to make sure you're not just reading their answers. You want to help participants elaborate on the most creative thoughts. For example, if you've asked, "What does a best boss do?" and Suku says, "Empower you," *don't* say, "Yes, they empower you." Instead ask, "What did that boss actually *do* to empower you?" This way, you make sure the participant is doing the talking and digging for deeper understanding.

Listen to All Voices.   Make sure you listen to all voices. You may want to keep a checklist (see Figure 10.5) to track how many times you have called on each participant and heard them talk. If possible, have all participants share at least twice: first after your introductory greeting and conversation, and again at the end when everyone goes around and shares their key learnings.

Tap into People's Strengths.   Each of us exhibits a combination of strengths or learning preferences. Howard Gardner talks about this in terms of "multiple intelligences." Virtual facilitators, who vary their teaching strategies, will enable learners to tap into their strengths and maximize their learning. The following list of ideas to consider for activities covers a range of strengths and is based on Gardner's Multiple Intelligences[3] (see Chapter 5 in this book for a more extensive explanation).

Name	√	√	√
Bubba	√		
Sharla	√	√	

Figure 10.5. Sample Learner Participation Checklist

Intrapersonal intelligence: Ability to self-reflect and be aware of one's inner state of being

Learners will like:

- Engaging their emotions
- Asking questions that delve into feelings, motivations, and fears
- Reflecting on impact of others on them
- Sharing how someone solved a problem

Interpersonal intelligence: Ability to relate to and understand another's/ multiple points of view

Learners will like:

- Talking in a private chat box with a partner
- Role-playing or doing skill practice in small groups
- Using polls to gather information and convey feelings
- Reflecting on chats and diving deeper

Verbal/Linguistic intelligence: Ability to use words and language

Learners will respond well to:

- Storytelling or listening to stories
- Case studies
- Interpreting text
- Chats

Naturalist intelligence: Ability to connect personally with nature

Learners will relate best to:

- Images of nature
- Outdoor activities

Visual/Spatial intelligence: Ability to perceive the visual

Learners will respond well to:

- Clear graphics
- Charts, maps, flowcharts
- Mind maps
- Annotating

Logical/Mathematical intelligence: Ability to use reason, logic, and numbers

Learners will enjoy:

- Setting up a matrix for goals for people to fill out
- Analyzing problems
- Developing theories
- Interviewing an expert or peer

Bodily/Kinesthetic intelligence: Ability to control/utilize the body and express oneself through movement

Learners will enjoy:

- Writing notes and creating charts
- Playing games such as *Name That Tune*, Highly Paid Experts, *Jeopardy*
- Annotating in a workbook
- Using Brain Gym[4] for a break. Ask all to stand up, stretch, touch their right elbow to their left knee five times and then reverse

Musical/Rhythmic intelligence: Ability to produce or appreciate music, think in sounds, rhythms, and patterns

Learners will respond well to:

- Singing a song to illustrate a concept
- Using songs that review or teach
- Trying sound effects
- Listening to baroque music while working

Existential intelligence: Ability to think "big picture" and theorize about life, death, love, and existence

Learners will relate best to:

- Philosophical discussions about life
- Theories of existence
- Pondering ultimate realities such as love and death
- How small things fit into the "big picture"

What's In It for YOU to Manage E-mail before It Manages YOU?

- ☑ To be calmer, more in control
- ☑ To have more time, less e-mail
- ☑ To improve your professional image
- ☑ To be able to focus on what is important to **YOU**

Figure 10.6. Example of Generating Meaning and Relevancy

Generate Meaning

You can help learners maintain a high level of commitment to participating and learning virtually if every 10 minutes or so you interject a question that asks participants to consider how this learning session benefits them. For example, try asking "What's in it for you to put this learning into action?" "Why is this important in your world?" "Where would you use this information?" "How does this relate to X" (where X is an organizational or personal issue)? "How will this help you do your job or achieve an aspiration?" "How does the learning enhance relevancy?" Asking these kinds of questions helps kick in and ignite an emotional connection or passion around the subject as well as the motivation to continue learning.

Apply to Real World

Real-world practice requires a high level of commitment on behalf of learners. By the time you get to their applying what they have just learned to their world, you are really having people "put it out there," and this may feel risky. Your job is to minimize risk and model application.

Begin with your more extroverted participants and the ones who have been speaking up, but move to a place where everyone gets to demonstrate how they've applied the learning to the real world. Your goal in this section is to show participants how applicable what they've just learned is in their real life and work, and that changing behavior takes an effort.

As each person demonstrates what they have learned, have others rate them and offer suggestions in the chat box. For example, if they are learning facilitation skills, you may have them actually demonstrate how they will use what they just learned in a presentation they are about to give. They

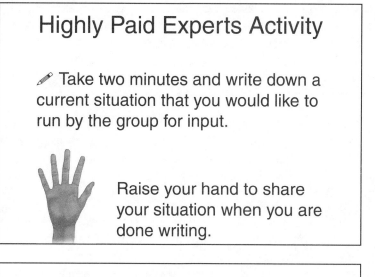

Highly Paid Experts Activity

✏ Take two minutes and write down a current situation that you would like to run by the group for input.

Raise your hand to share your situation when you are done writing.

Walk the Walk Exercise

- Create an A-B-C e-mail for a colleague who needs help.
- Share what you learned today.
- Create a strong subject line, a brief, warm greeting, and a sculpted A-B-C body.
- Type it on a whiteboard and prepare to share with us.

Figure 10.7. Example of Applying Learning to Real World
(Excerpted from Song, Halsey, and Burress, *The Hamster Revolution*.[5])

might role-play, then share and get feedback from others about what they liked as well as what they would add. In another exercise, a participant shares a relevant, current situation and asks a group of "Highly Paid Experts" to share their thoughts from their new learning. The participant requesting advice uses the whiteboard, and the "experts" give input in the chat box.

Gauge and Celebrate

All virtual calls or sessions should end with a global review, quiz, or assessment that demonstrates to learners how much they've learned in the short time they have been in the session with you. These quizzes can take many forms: a multiple-choice, true/false, or fill-in-the-blank test; a crossword puzzle; or a *Jeopardy* or other type of quiz game. It can be anything that's quick but makes them realize that when they signed on they didn't know this information but now they have learned it.

Buddy Up. Assign learning buddies to participants (or have them choose their own), and ask them to share their goal with each other in the chat box. Have them exchange phone numbers and e-mail addresses in a private chat with their buddy. Recommend that they contact each other within 72 hours and talk about how they are doing on their goals.

Share Key Learnings. Using your participant checklist, ask everyone to share the most important learning they have had from the session. After they have shared their learning, involve them further by having them state their commitment to using this learning. Have everyone type in the chat box one way they are going to use that key learning in their life, either before the next session or in general.

End Session on Time. It is very important that you start and stop virtual sessions on time so people can keep their other commitments. Typically, people schedule their learning sessions between other meetings, so it is optimal to start and stop on time. This will avoid having people sign on and off at varying times, which can be very distracting to participants.

Extend Learning to Action

You can do many things to help learners extend their learning and apply it beyond the learning event. Here are some examples:

- Publish success stories as internal marketing tools.
- Offer mini-refreshers on microbehaviors that will enable participants to put learnings into practice.

- Hold reunions and gather stories.

- E-mail a post-test one to two weeks after classes, and award prizes such as gift cards or other small gifts.

- Give awards for best user as recommended by peers.

- Provide mentors. Choose a few stars to log on to the next class, give testimonials on how good the course was, and offer to serve as mentors.

- Conduct an e-mail or face-to-face survey: how has the learning been applied on the job? (This will help you learn what follow-up people need and want.)

- Gather return on investment (ROI) data via phone or e-mail survey. Ask for and measure ROI where the training made an impact on business objectives. Consolidate this into a short report to send to executives and other sponsors.

- Hold lunch phone-call review sessions where you ask for success stories and review challenges.

- Get a coach. Have someone help you act on your best intentions.[6]

REFLECTION: Exercise

VIRTUAL FACILITATION VERSUS CLASSROOM FACILITATION

- What do you *do* to bring out the brilliance in face-to-face sessions?

- What do you *need* to bring out the brilliance virtually?

  - Even greater listening skills

  - Extremely clear directions

  - The ability to multitask

(Continued)

- Energy and joy

- Succinct explanations of content

- Quick, deep activities to keep reengaging

- (What else would you add?)

A Legacy of Learning

A good teacher, speaker, coach—anyone imparting wisdom, influencing people, and believing in their brilliance—can help turn a life around, and that is an awesome prospect. As I think about that possibility, I think of Enrique, a young boy from Mexico who was adopted by one of my former MSEL students. Enrique was struggling in school. His teacher and his parents couldn't reach him. They were at the end of their rope because no matter what they tried they could not get Enrique to sit still and do his schoolwork. Thinking that he might be more successful in a school in Mexico, Enrique's parents were considering sending him there to live with extended family. In class one night, we talked about multiple learning styles. As I described characteristics of kinesthetic learners and gave examples of how they learn best, Enrique's dad sat taking notes. A light went on for him as he thought about his son. My student went home and talked to his wife, and they started trying with Enrique some of the strategies we'd talked about. They had him jump on a mini-trampoline while practicing his spelling words and clap out his math problems. They encouraged him to walk around the house while reviewing his science notes. It worked: Enrique began to happily do his work and succeed in school. Needless to say, his parents were overjoyed that they wouldn't have

Celebrating with Cohort 10 from the MSEL Program at University of San Diego.

to resort to sending him away. I knew nothing of this until one night at class Enrique's father showed me a photo of his son and said, "You saved our family."

Whose life might you inadvertently change for the better by sharing your knowledge? The enduring impact of a lesson taught well is endless. You never know which story, activity, or question will be the kernel of wisdom that triggers an epiphany and propels change. You never know when the cumulative experience of impactful learning will make it impossible for someone's life to ever be the same. Your ability to build communities of spirited, capable, confident learners can be the spark that sets in motion a chain of hope and enthusiasm that transforms lives. It only takes one—*one* person in *one* of your learning experiences—to find his or her voice and serve as a catalyst who rallies a team, a community, an organization, or even a nation to take on the most imposing human problems and make the world a better place.

What is it you hope to accomplish through your teaching and in your sphere of influence? Do you hope to change the world? As you seek to transform lives through learning, teach as though each life you touch could be the one to end world hunger or to generate an idea that brings about world peace. Celebrate each teachable moment, each learner's victories. They are your brightest moments—the potential turning points in the learning journey. They are your legacy. And they *do* transform lives.

> Let us think of education as the means of developing our greatest abilities, because in each of us there is a private hope and dream which, fulfilled, can be translated into benefit for everyone and greater strength of the nation.
>
> —John F. Kennedy

Free Assessment—The Building Excellence Survey

Know How You Best Learn

How do you best learn? How do you best take in information, process it, and retain it? This would be a great time to take an amazing assessment donated to this book from PCI Learn (www.learningstyles.net) called The Building Excellence Survey.

The authors of this instrument (which my university students have wondered how they lived their whole lives without) have identified 28 different elements that can affect each person uniquely. Thus, when you take The Building Excellence Survey and print your report, you will learn which of the 28 elements will trigger concentration, maintain it, and cause you to produce long-term memory and retention. It is important to know that your learning style, *which often is your teaching style,* is based on a complex set of reactions to varied stimuli, both biologically inherited traits and previously established behavioral patterns. The assessment will not only give you knowledge about your preferences, but will depict the range of preferences of the people you seek to influence. Have fun using this *one-time only* opportunity to learn how you learn. (If you want to give others the opportunity to take this great assessment, it is only $5.00 from the Web site.)

Taking the Building Excellence Survey

- Access the Web site: www.learningstyles.net
- Click **Free Sign Up** at the top
- Complete the form and click the **Submit** button
- Click on **My Assessments** at the top

- Enter Account Code: **2XAZA** in the box (Code expires 12/31/2013)
- Select your language then click the **Launch Survey** button
- Follow the instructions, take the BE Survey, and then print your report

From the author of the Building Excellence Survey:

It is an honor and a privilege to offer the Building Excellence (BE) Survey to each individual who purchases a copy of Brilliance by Design. I have known Vicki Halsey for over ten years. Her energy, spirit, and outstanding skills as a leader, trainer, and writer make this all worthwhile.

Although how humans learn is a complex subject, there is one basic, undeniable assumption—one size does not fit all. Everyone has strengths and preferences in learning and working settings. The importance of identifying learning style is that it not only provides each person (child or adult) with his or her unique set of strengths, it provides teachers and trainers with an organized approach for the application of individualized instruction in the classroom or training room. This includes providing the right setting and various other aspects of learning environments related to improved achievement, behaviors, and attitudes toward learning. At the heart of educational institutions and workplace settings are learning individuals who breathe life into concepts that evolve into promise for the future. When individuals succeed, everyone triumphs.

—Susan M. Rundle

President of Performance Concepts International, Director of the International Learning Styles Network (ILSN), and co-author of the Building Excellence (BE) Survey (Rundle, S. and Dunn, R. 1996–2008)

REFLECTION: Review

BUILDING EXCELLENCE SURVEY REFLECTIONS

What I learned about me as a learner includes:

How this knowledge will impact my teaching includes:

Getting Started Creating Brilliance by Design

I am not a teacher, but an awakener.
—Robert Frost

So by now you're probably ready to jump in and start creating your own sessions using the principles, strategies, and tips from *Brilliance by Design*. To get started, let's think for a minute about your core purpose. Are you going to run a meeting or create a workshop? Let's dive into each one of these.

Running a Meeting

1. **People:** Who are the people coming to the meeting? What do they hope to gain by attending this meeting? What do you know about them? What is going on in their world that might impact how they show up? Are the right decision makers invited to the meeting?

2. **Content:** What is your objective for the meeting? What agenda do you want to follow? When the people walk out the door, what are you hoping they will achieve? What do you want people to do first? What handouts will you be giving them?

3. **Learning Design: The ENGAGE Model**

Running a Meeting	
E—Energize Learners	• What will you do to give learners a heads up as to what's going to go on at the meeting? • Will you send them an e-mail, give them a handwritten letter, or send them a little gift to excite them about what's going to happen? • What pre-work will you send them so they can start thinking about what you're going to talk about? • In preparation for the meeting, think about the energy-building, protein snacks you may have for them. • How will the environment be set up?
N—Navigate Content	• What idea for interactivity will you use to open your meeting? • Will you use a key question to draw from them what they are hoping for or what they thought because of the pre-learning material? • Will you use a mind map or graphics organizer? • How will you introduce/teach the content that you want to navigate? • Will you use lectures? Stories? • Will you use a cooperative learning strategy where you have them teach each other? • What activities will you use to have them do deep practice with what you are teaching? • Will you use any case studies?
G—Generate Meaning	• What will you do to generate meaning and ask for the benefits, or the value, of what they are learning, processing, and constructing in terms of their knowledge about it?
A—Apply to Real World	• How will you have people at the meeting apply what they learn in their day-to-day life? • What will you do to have them create a move-forward action plan or to determine next steps?

189

G—Gauge and Celebrate	• How will you show them how much they have learned in this meeting?
	• What type of assessments will you give?
	• Will you create a crossword puzzle, a mini-quiz, a *Jeopardy* game, a multiple-choice test, or perhaps have them do a group mind map?
E—Extend Learning to Action	• How will you extend the learning to action?
	• What follow-up strategies will you use for your meeting? Will you do an e-fresher?
	• Will you write an e-mail thank-you note?
	• How will you bring people back together to share what they've done with what they learned at the meeting, and how they have moved forward and acted on their next steps?

Designing a Workshop

1. **People:** Who are the people attending your workshop? Why are they there? What are they hoping for? What are their objectives for attending the class? What's going on in their world right now that might impact their learning? What is their comfort level with the way you are teaching (virtual, face-to-face, or blended)? What is their willingness to learn this new content? How will you ready yourself for this learning? What else do you know about them that might be important as you seek to unleash their brilliance?

2. **Content:** What amount of time do you have to teach your content? What are the main principles you want people to learn? What is the model you want to share, or what are your three to five key learnings? What do you want them to be able to do when they walk out the door?

3. **Learning Design: The ENGAGE Model**

Designing a Workshop	
E—Energize Learners	• What will you send out ahead of time to energize learners about the upcoming session? • How will you market the outcome participants are hoping for? • Will you e-mail, send a handwritten invitation, send testimonials from prior workshop participants? • Will you send pre-work such as a book or study guide? Will you send questions so they can interview other people around the topic? • How will you set up the room? • What healthy protein snacks will you have? • Will you change the lighting or have music playing upon their arrival? • Will you have posters or quotes on the wall?
N—Navigate Content	• What is your one-sentence overview of what people are going to learn? • What are the three main concepts you're going to teach to navigate your content? • How will you introduce these concepts—by lecture, video, activity, flip chart, or discussion? • What interaction/activities will you have? • Will you have them create questions and teach each other in a mini-teach? • Where will you tell or solicit powerful stories and anecdotes? • Review/Practice: Will you do a card sort, a case study, a video assessment, or a fill-in-the-blank review?

G—Generate Meaning	• What activity will you use to generate the meaning?
	• Will you do a flip chart "Benefit to me/the team/the organization" activity?
	• Will you ask them to write/discuss "What did I learn, and what is the value for me?" at their table or on a flip chart or whiteboard?
	• Will you have them calculate the value or dollarize the learning? Or ask them to assess: "What did I learn, and how will it add value in terms of achievement of business outcome?"
A—Apply to Real World	• How will you ask participants to do the exact behaviors you want from them after they finish the class?
	• How will you have them practice or role-play the exact behaviors you want?
	• What specific interactive activities will you do such as partner/peer observer learning lab, "Highly Paid Experts" activity, or role-play?
G—Gauge and Celebrate	• How will you show them how much they learned?
	• What will you do to have them celebrate their learning?
	• Will you use crossword puzzle knowledge tests, multiple-choice tests, or have them create a test? Will you play Stump the Panel, create a song, or make a newsletter?
E—Extend Learning to Action	• How will you facilitate creation of a support network and moving forward?
	• What strategies are you going to use for multiple touch points down the road to help people act on their best intentions?
	• Will you do a Lunch and Learn, e-freshers, podcasts, one-on-one coaching, "Who's Your Buddy," phone follow-up class, success-story generator, or a contest for the newsletter?

Do-It-Yourself Templates

Model Creation
DO-IT-YOURSELF TEMPLATE

1 What is (are) your big idea(s)?

_____
_____
_____

2 What do you want people to be able to do when they are done learning your content?

_____
_____
_____
_____
_____
_____
_____
_____
_____
_____
_____
_____

3 What are the 3 to 6 key themes, main ideas, principles, parts, skills, or behaviors that will enable people to do step 2?

_____
_____
_____
_____
_____

4 From your themes (step 3), what words trigger your big idea (step 1)?

_____   _____   _____
_____   _____   _____ .

Choose words to put in boxes below and chronologically create steps from your key concepts.

Words   **Steps**

[   ]   _____
[   ]   _____
[   ]   _____
[   ]   _____
[   ]   _____
[   ]   _____
[   ]   _____

E	• Energize Learners
N	• Navigate Content
G	• Generate Meaning
A	• Apply to Real World
G	• Gauge and Celebrate
E	• Extend Learning to Action

Energize Learners
DO-IT-YOURSELF TEMPLATE

PRE-SESSION

_____
_____
_____
_____
_____
_____
_____
_____
_____
_____
_____
_____
_____
_____
_____
_____
_____

❏ Personal invitation
❏ Welcome letter
❏ E-mail invite
❏ Pre-interview questions
❏ Senior leader endorsement
❏ Journey map/learner map/agenda in pictures
❏ Timeline
❏ Preassessment
❏ Book or article
❏ Study guides
❏ Questions to think about
❏ Podcast
❏ Prerecorded webinar
❏ Impact map
❏ Testimonials from previous participants
❏ Video/DVD
❏ Inspirational quotes
" _____ "

STARTING THE SESSION

_____
_____
_____
_____
_____
_____
_____
_____
_____
_____
_____
_____
_____

❏ Energizing environment/novelty
   ❏ Toys for kinesthetic, pens, etc.
   ❏ Protein snacks, water
❏ Quotes, posters, visuals
❏ Music
❏ Greeting each participant and learning two facts
❏ Getting participants talking early
❏ Asking catchy opening question
" _____ "

❏ Initial activity/active participation
❏ Value statement to participants
" _____ "

❏ Key objectives/themes for the day
❏ My promise to you is: _____
❏ K/W/L chart

E	• Energize Learners
N	• **Navigate Content**
G	• Generate Meaning
A	• Apply to Real World
G	• Gauge and Celebrate
E	• Extend Learning to Action

Navigate Content

DO-IT-YOURSELF TEMPLATE

What core information, ideas, and/or takeaways are you hoping to impart?

❏ _____

❏ _____

❏ _____

❏ _____

What research will you share?

_____

_____

_____

What is your opening Total Active Involvement (TAI) idea, question, or activity?

_____

_____

_____

What beliefs do you want participants leaving with to ensure long-term behavior change?

_____

_____

_____

How will you introduce them to the content?

❏ Demonstrate/model
❏ Lecture and slides
❏ Cooperative learning/Jigsaw
❏ Discussion
❏ Guest speaker

❏ Experience, then label
❏ Video/DVD
❏ Written information (handouts)
❏ Stories to share

What activities will help people actively learn, review content, and have Total Intense Participation?

❏ Card sort/matching game
❏ Mind map/graphic organizer
❏ Scenario analysis
❏ Case study
❏ Role-play
❏ Flash cards

❏ Game/puzzle/mnemonic
❏ Multiple-choice/fill-in/true-or-false quiz
❏ Participants teach each other
❏ Think/pair/share
❏ Mini-teach
❏ Video analysis

VISUAL

❏ Images versus work
❏ Color/images
❏ Vivid stories
❏ Mind map
❏ Job aid/one-page synthesis

AUDITORY

❏ Talk with a partner
❏ Describe flow
❏ Recording/podcasts
❏ Listen to lecture/discussion

KINESTHETIC

❏ Puzzle with manipulatives
❏ Flip chart activity
❏ Building the model
❏ Four Corners review (answers in four corners)
❏ Teach a partner

E	• Energize Learners
N	**• Navigate Content**
G	• Generate Meaning
A	• Apply to Real World
G	• Gauge and Celebrate
E	• Extend Learning to Action

Navigate Content

DO-IT-YOURSELF TEMPLATE

What story/stories will you tell that will tap into emotions and ignite interest about the concept?

_____

_____

_____

MULTIPLE INTELLIGENCES: Help People BE Smart

Verbal/Linguistic
- ❏ Stories
- ❏ Retelling key themes
- ❏ Reading case study
- ❏ Demonstrating

Visual/Spatial
- ❏ Images/charts/posters
- ❏ Building a model/visual depiction
- ❏ Illustrating

Interpersonal
- ❏ Peer teaching
- ❏ Team activities
- ❏ Cooperative learning

Intrapersonal
- ❏ Reflection time/journaling
- ❏ Personal action planning/goal setting

Musical/Rhythmic
- ❏ Creating a song with the topic
- ❏ Musical welcome and while working

Bodily/Kinesthetic
- ❏ Hands-on experiments
- ❏ Arranging puzzle pieces
- ❏ Role-play/skill practice

Logical/Mathematical
- ❏ Visual charts, data
- ❏ Experimentation
- ❏ Coding or sequencing information

Naturalist
- ❏ Pictures of nature in slide
- ❏ Walking outside for 10 minutes of teach/share

Existential
- ❏ Discussing how small learnings fit into bigger picture
- ❏ Philosophical discussions

E	• Energize Learners
N	• Navigate Content
G	**• Generate Meaning**
A	• Apply to Real World
G	• Gauge and Celebrate
E	• Extend Learning to Action

Generate Meaning
DO-IT-YOURSELF TEMPLATE

When will you ask to generate their understanding of the benefits/relevancy of the content to their world/achievement of their goals?

❏ _____	❏ _____	❏ _____
_____	_____	_____
_____	_____	_____

ACTIVITY: ❏ Flip Chart
            ❏ Poster

BENEFITS TO:

ME	TEAM	ORGANIZATION

What have you learned?	What does it mean?

E	• Energize Learners
N	• Navigate Content
G	• Generate Meaning
A	**• Apply to Real World**
G	• Gauge and Celebrate
E	• Extend Learning to Action

Apply to Real World

DO-IT-YOURSELF TEMPLATE

Skills I want people to apply include:

_____

_____

_____

_____

_____

_____

If people could . . .

❑ _____

❑ _____

❑ _____

❑ _____

❑ _____

. . . after the learning process, it would create optimal results.

To help people apply their learning, I will use the following strategies:

❑ Create a checklist to enable feedback.

❑ Create a learning lab.

❑ Facilitate a cross-training session.

❑ Apply team analysis.

❑ Create a scenario.

❑ Apply a mini–case study.

❑ Record a video encounter.

❑ Act out a system.

❑ Role-play or perform skill practice.

❑ Use an action learning exercise.

❑ Initiate problem solving.

❑ Use a Highly Paid Experts activity.

❑ Create a clear "next steps" action plan.

❑ Create a support network.

To have people show themselves the value of applying the new skills and techniques, I will:

_____

_____

E	• Energize Learners
N	• Navigate Content
G	• Generate Meaning
A	• Apply to Real World
G	**• Gauge and Celebrate**
E	• Extend Learning to Action

Gauge and Celebrate

DO-IT-YOURSELF TEMPLATE

What will you do to have learners review and celebrate all they've learned while moving concepts from short-term memory to long-term memory?

What do you want to assess? _____

_____

_____

_____

_____

Which strategies would work best for you?

❏ Differentiate questions moving up Bloom's taxonomy.

❏ Create a group mind map.

❏ Play 3–2–1.

❏ Write a song.

❏ Stump the Panel (each learner makes 5 questions).

❏ Make a newsletter/newspaper headlines.

❏ Share one key learning.

❏ Create an acronym.

❏ Create 5 visible signs flip chart.

❏ Play Koosh ball review.

❏ Play *Jeopardy*/game show.

❏ Do crossword puzzle review.

❏ Design your own model from new information.

❏ Give multiple-choice test.

❏ Give matching test.

❏ Give true/false test.

❏ Give short answer test.

❏ Combination of the above.

E	• Energize Learners
N	• Navigate Content
G	• Generate Meaning
A	• Apply to Real World
G	• Gauge and Celebrate
E	• Extend Learning to Action

Extend Learning to Action
DO-IT-YOURSELF TEMPLATE

What else would extend the learning and help people act on their best intentions?

❑ E-mail reminders

❑ Coaching

❑ Success case studies/stories

❑ Business impact contest—dollarize—show results in action

❑ Giving each person a buddy

❑ Getting manager involved

❑ Letter to self—mailing a letter they wrote themselves with their intentions

❑ Awards contests for best use

❑ Podcast follow-ups

❑ E-freshers in virtual classrooms

❑ User teams

❑ Mentor from a previous class

❑ Job aids as a reminder

❑ Phone review sessions

❑ Posters with key model, strategies

❑ "Tip of the Week"

❑ Lunch and Learns

❑ Video contest

❑ Interviews with stars in newsletter

❑ Peer nominations for awards

❑ Individual coaches

❑ Team support group

Notes

Introduction: The Time for Brilliance Has Come

1. Martin Kornacki, "Workers Value Professional Training But Are Unhappy with What Employers Provide," *Training Journal,* February 2, 2006, www.trainingjournal.com/news/2753.html (accessed August 2010).

Chapter 1: Fire Up the Synergy between Learners and Teachers

1. Dale Chihuly's Web site, www.chihuly.com/intro.html.
2. *Webster's New World Dictionary* (New York: Simon & Schuster, 1982), 1444.
3. Wikipedia, "Synergy," http://en.wikipedia.org/wiki/Synergy (accessed February 2010).
4. Thomas Friedman, "Foreign Affairs; My Favorite Teacher," *New York Times,* January 9, 2001, www.nytimes.com/2001/01/09/opinion/foreign-affairs-my-favorite-teacher.html (accessed August 2010).
5. Kevin Cashman, *Leadership from the Inside Out: Becoming a Leader for Life* (San Francisco: Berrett-Koehler, 2008), 80.
6. Bill George and Peter Sims, *True North: Discover Your Authentic Leadership* (San Francisco: Jossey-Bass, 2007), 82–83.
7. George and Sims, *True North,* 174–179.
8. Layne Cutright and Paul Cutright, *You're Never Upset for the Reason You Think* (Las Vegas: Heart to Heart, 2004), 151–158.

Chapter 2: Craft Content That Sings

1. Bennett Cerf and Van H. Cartmell, eds., *The Best Short Stories of O. Henry* (New York: Modern Library, 1994), 1–6; Kahlil Gibran, *The Prophet* (New York: Alfred A. Knopf, 1980), 19–22.
2. Hyrum W. Smith, *What Matters Most: The Power of Living Your Value* (New York: Fireside, 2001).
3. Daniel Coyle, *The Talent Code: Greatness Isn't Born, It's Grown. Here's How* (New York: Bantam Dell, 2009), 5, 6, 32, 33, 38, 39.

Chapter 3: The ENGAGE Model: An Overview

1. Coyle, *The Talent Code,* 40, 69–73.

Chapter 4: Energize Learners

1. Coyle, *The Talent Code,* 40–46.

2. Rob Brinkerhoff, *The Success Case Method: Find Out Quickly What's Working and What's Not* (San Francisco: Berrett-Koehler, 2003).

3. For more information on Impact Mapping, we recommend: www.proveandimprove .org/new/getst/ImpactMap.php (accessed August 2010).

4. Susan Rundle, www.learningstyles.net (accessed June 2010).

5. Coyle, *The Talent Code*, 102–106.

6. Cashman, *Leadership from the Inside Out*, 100.

Chapter 5: Navigate Content

1. If you would like to see an example of how I teach this, go to www.kenblanchard.com/ News_Events/Leadership_Management_Webinars/Archived_Webinars, and click on my archived webinar, *Managing and Helping People to Be Their Best*.

2. *TrustWorks* is a program of The Ken Blanchard Companies, www.blanchardlearning .com/templates/group.asp?group=646 (accessed September 2010).

3. Howard Gardner, *Frames of Mind: The Theory of Multiple Intelligences* (New York: Basic Books, 1993).

4. The Web sites for Marcus Buckingham are www.tmbc.com and www.marcusbuckingham .com.

5. The Web sites for Keith Ferrazzi are www.ferrazzigreenlight.com and www.keithferrazzi .com.

6. The Web site for Tony Buzan is www.thinkbuzan.com.

7. Juanita Brown and David Isaacs, *The World Café: Shaping Our Futures through Conversations That Matter* (San Francisco: Berrett-Koehler, 2005), 174–175.

8. David Garvin's video case studies are available via the Harvard Business School Press, at http://hbr.org/search/David%25252520Garvin%25252520Learning%25252520 Organization%25252520DVD/ (accessed August 2010).

9. James Flaherty, *Coaching: Evoking Excellence in Others* (Burlington, MA: Butterworth-Heinemann, 2010).

Chapter 6: Generate Meaning

1. Coyle, *The Talent Code*, 32–38.

2. William R. Miller and Stephen Rollnick, *Motivational Interviewing: Preparing People for Change* (New York: Guilford Press, 2002), 3–4.

3. Eric Jensen, *The Learning Brain* (San Diego: Brain Store, 1994), 53.

Chapter 7: Apply to Real World

1. Keith Ferrazzi and Tahl Raz, *Never Eat Alone: And Other Secrets to Success One Relationship at a Time* (New York: Broadway Business, 2005).

Chapter 8: Gauge and Celebrate

1. Wikipedia, "Bloom's Taxonomy," http://en.wikipedia.org/wiki/Bloom's Taxonomy (accessed June 2010).

2. Benjamin S. Bloom, *Taxonomy of Educational Objectives, Handbook 1: Cognitive Domain* (Reading, MA: Addison Wesley, 1956).

3. John Medina, *Brain Rules: 12 Rules for Surviving and Thriving in Work, Home, and School* (Seattle: Pear Press, 2009), 95, 212.

Chapter 9: Extend Learning to Action

1. Cal Wick, Roy Pollock, and Andy Jefferson, "The New Finish Line for Learning," *T+D Magazine,* July 2009, 64–69; www.forthillcompany.com/wp-content/uploads/td-article-063009.pdf (accessed August 2010).

2. Mike Song, Vicki Halsey, and Tim Burress, *The Hamster Revolution: How to Manage Your Email before It Manages You* (San Francisco: Berrett-Koehler, 2007), 36.

3. Jack Zenger, Joe Folkman, and Robert Sherwin, "The Promise of Phase 3," *Training and Development* (January 2005), 31–34.

Chapter 10: Bringing Out Brilliance in the Virtual Classroom

1. The following Web sites and books on emotional intelligence are excellent resources, and there are many others: Institute for Health and Human Potential, "What Is EQ?" www.ihhp.com/what_is_eq.htm (accessed August 2010); Daniel Goleman, "Emotional Intelligence," www.danielgoleman.info/topics/emotional-intelligence/ (accessed August 2010); Travis Bradbury and Jean Reeves, EQ 2.0 (San Diego: TalentSmart, 2009); and Daniel Goleman, *Working with Emotional Intelligence* (New York: Bantam, 1998).

2. Eric Jensen, *Superteaching: Over 1000 Practical Strategies* (Thousand Oaks, CA: Corwin Press, 1995).

3. Gardner, *Frames of Mind.*

4. Brain Gym Web site, www.braingym.com.

5. This illustration is from the workbook that accompanies Song, Halsey, and Burress, *The Hamster Revolution.*

6. For more information on coaching, see The Ken Blanchard Companies Web site at www.coaching.com.

Bibliography

Blanchard, Ken. *Leading at a Higher Level: Blanchard on Leadership and Creating High Performing Organizations.* Upper Saddle River, NJ: F.T. Press, 2009.

Bloom, Benjamin S. *Taxonomy of Educational Objectives, Handbook 1: Cognitive Domain.* Reading, MA: Addison Wesley, 1956.

Bradbury, Travis, and Jean Reeves. *EQ 2.0.* San Diego: TalentSmart, 2009.

Brinkerhoff, Robert O. *The Success Case Method: Find Out Quickly What's Working and What's Not.* San Francisco: Berrett-Koehler, 2003.

Brown, Juanita, and David Isaacs. *The World Café: Shaping Our Futures through Conversations That Matter.* San Francisco: Berrett-Koehler, 2005.

Cashman, Kevin. *Leadership from the Inside Out: Becoming a Leader for Life.* San Francisco: Berrett-Koehler, 2008.

Coyle, Daniel. *The Talent Code: Greatness Isn't Born, It's Grown. Here's How.* New York: Bantam Dell, 2009.

Cutright, Layne, and Paul Cutright. *You're Never Upset for the Reason You Think.* Las Vegas: Heart to Heart, 2004.

Eikenberry, Kevin. *Remarkable Leadership: Unleashing Your Leadership Potential One Skill at a Time.* San Francisco: Jossey-Bass, 2007.

Ferrazzi, Keith, and Tahl Raz. *Never Eat Alone: And Other Secrets to Success One Relationship at a Time.* New York: Broadway Business, 2005.

Flaherty, James. *Coaching: Evoking Excellence in Others.* Burlington, MA: Butterworth-Heinemann, 2010.

Freiberg, Kevin, and Jackie. *Boom! 7 Choices for Blowing the Doors Off Business-As-Usual.* Nashville, TN: Thomas Nelson, 2007.

Gardner, Howard. *Frames of Mind: The Theory of Multiple Intelligences.* New York: Basic Books, 1993.

George, Bill, and Peter Sims. *True North: Discover Your Authentic Leadership.* San Francisco: Jossey-Bass, 2007.

Gladwell, Malcolm. *What the Dog Saw and Other Adventures.* New York: Little, Brown, 2009.

Goleman, Daniel. *Working with Emotional Intelligence.* New York: Bantam, 1998.

Jensen, Eric. *The Learning Brain.* San Diego: Brain Store, 1994.

———. *Superteaching: Over 1000 Practical Strategies.* Thousand Oaks, CA: Corwin Press, 1995.

Medina, John. *Brain Rules: 12 Rules for Surviving and Thriving in Work, Home, and School.* Seattle: Pear Press, 2009.

Meier, David. *The Accelerated Learning Handbook: A Creative Guide to Designing and Delivering Faster, More Effective Training Programs.* New York: McGraw-Hill, 2000.

Miller, William R., and Stephen Rollnick. *Motivational Interviewing: Preparing People for Change.* New York: Guilford Press, 2002.

Pearce, Howard. *The Owner's Manual to the Brain: Everyday Applications from Mind-Brain Research.* Austin, TX: Bard, 2006.

Rock, David, and Jeffrey Schwartz. "The Neuroscience of Leadership." *Strategy + Business* 43, May 30, 2006. www.strategy-business.com/article/06207.

Rose, Colin. *Master It Faster: How to Learn Faster, Make Good Decisions and Think Creatively.* Aylesbury, Buckinghamshire, United Kingdom: Accelerated Learning Systems, 2000.

Smith, Hyrum W. *What Matters Most: The Power of Living Your Value.* New York: Fireside, 2001.

Song, Mike, Vicki Halsey, and Tim Burress. *The Hamster Revolution: How to Manage Your Email before It Manages You.* San Francisco: Berrett-Koehler, 2007.

———. *The Hamster Revolution for Meetings: How to Meet Less and Get More Done.* San Francisco: Berrett-Koehler, 2009.

Acknowledgments

Everything in this book I have learned from someone. My life has been so blessed by the honest, generous, open, and powerful friends who have changed and enhanced my life. I cannot thank each of you enough for sharing your care, love, and brilliance, but I thought I would try to acknowledge what I believe is the greatest gift I have learned from each of you.

Rick Halsey:	Value yourself and stand up for your principles.
Nick Halsey:	Be vigilant with my words and laugh often.
Jake Halsey:	Compromise and conviction are a powerful combination.
Elaine White:	Never give up. Tenacity is the key to success.
Lisa Smedley:	Lifelong friends are the anchors of dreams.
Kate Orf:	Connect, laugh often, and generously share.
Ken Blanchard:	Friends, passion, stories, and catching people doing something right are the secrets to success in life.
Margie Blanchard:	Keep on learning. Believing in someone and acting on that belief is an unbeatable catalyst for change.
Debbie Blanchard:	Be aware, release your inner strength, and always share the love.

Scott Blanchard:	A passionate depiction of data goes a long way to help people to listen to brilliance.
Madeleine Homan Blanchard:	Fewer words equal a more transformational message.
Pat Zigarmi:	Give people a chance, support their early learning, and stand up for what you believe in.
Kathy Cuff:	Love your family and speak from the heart.
Jennifer Zingg:	A great, prepared teacher inspires, energizes, and is a miracle to have.
Renee Broadwell:	Be excited to live, find joy in everything you do, and notice the good.
Bob Lorber:	Listen to and love your friends; they are what makes life worthwhile.
Margie Adler:	Encourage the heart, listen with acuity, and patiently integrate brilliance.
Martha Lawrence:	Seek peace, share, and clarify. Remember, words can change the world.
Susie Houle:	Be creative; it fuels creativity.
Charlotte Jordan:	Play to your strengths, choose your words carefully, and be ready to laugh at all times.
Nancy Jordan:	Peace begins with me.
Raz Ingrasci:	You are not your patterns. You are the light.
Howard Farfel:	Be spontaneous, clear, curious, and persistent.
Colin Rose:	Spark a love of lifelong learning and help people to "Master It Faster."
Su Ramsey:	Stick with your friends—they give you great strength.

Keith Ferrazzi:	Relationships drive life and give it meaning. Follow through.
Marcus Buckingham:	Strengths energize and open you up to the life you are meant to live.
Kevin Small:	Connect people; the synergy will change the world.
Linda Miller:	Gain permission to share and act on your values.
Warren Bennis:	Leadership is conversation by conversation.
James Flaherty:	You see things because you can describe them.
Pierce Howard:	The brain is complex; knowledge of the brain can help you create a life well lived.
Bill Foster:	There is great strength in gentleness.
Sue Daughters:	Inspire with grace and love.

Proud graduates ready to unleash their brilliance on the world!

Jean Beverage:	Courage, curiosity, and love can change the world.
Marshall Goldsmith:	Tackle one thing at a time, get help from others, and always answer your e-mail.
Mike Song:	Books can be written and change the world, one model at a time.
Karl Bimshas:	*Brilliance by Design* is a great title.
Marta Brooks:	Living in service to others is a life well lived.
Sarah Caverhill:	People remember short, clear, powerful messages.
Joe Ross:	Leadership is a discipline.
Colleen Barrett:	To care simply, and simply care.
My MSEL and EMBA Students:	Leadership, learning, and teaching have a symbiotic relationship in making the world a better place, person by person.
Cooper Halsey:	Make everyone feel like a rock star, and ask for what you need.

Thank you all for awakening my spirit and teaching me to love learning.

Photographers:	Jason Moorhead and Rick Halsey
Graphic artist:	Jane R. Griffith

Index

About the Author

Vicki Halsey, Ph.D.
Speaker, Author, Consultant, Trainer, Coach

Vicki Halsey is a spirited inspirational speaker, author, and compulsive teacher who energizes audiences worldwide by engaging their hearts as well as their minds. Her diverse résumé includes over twenty years as a public school teacher, counselor, and school administrator. For the last fifteen years she has joyously served as Vice President of Applied Learning for The Ken Blanchard Companies, where she writes, facilitates, coaches, and gives keynote speeches in an effort to help people claim their greatness.

Vicki, a national champion platform diver, loves the rigor and practice needed to develop talent. She partners with organizations such as Nike, Pfizer, Microsoft, Gap, Procter and Gamble, Wells Fargo, and many more to develop their people through interactive workshops, keynotes, webinars, and numerous other classroom and e-learning experiences. She is the coauthor of Blanchard's Legendary Customer Service Training as well their award-winning blended e-learning Situational Leadership® II program. In addition, Vicki crafted the highly acclaimed MSEL and EMBA degree programs for the University of San Diego and Grand Canyon University, respectively.

As an instructional designer, Vicki creates a power boost for the cutting-edge content of well-known management gurus such as Marcus Buckingham, Keith Ferrazzi, and Ken Blanchard by infusing their work with optimal learning practices and innovative training materials. *Brilliance by Design* is a direct result of the work she has done with hundreds of brilliant authors and subject matter experts.

Vicki has coauthored *Leading at a Higher Level* with Ken Blanchard and other consulting partners and founding associates, as well as *The Hamster Revolution: How to Manage Your Email before It Manages You* and *The Hamster Revolution for Meetings: How to Meet Less and Get More Done,* both with Mike Song and Tim Burress.

Vicki, her wonderful husband Rick, and their sons Nick and Jake happily live in San Diego. To contact Vicki about a workshop or keynote address, please call 760-739-6917 or e-mail vicki.halsey@kenblanchard.com.

Services Available from The Ken Blanchard Companies

The Ken Blanchard Companies® is a global leader in workplace learning, productivity, performance, and leadership effectiveness that is best known for its Situational Leadership® II program—the most widely taught leadership model in the world. Because of its ability to help people excel as self-leaders and as leaders of others, SLII® is embraced by Fortune 500 companies as well as midsize to small-size businesses, governments, and educational and non-profit organizations.

Blanchard® programs, which are based on the evidence that people are the key to accomplishing strategic objectives and driving business results, develop excellence in leadership, teams, customer loyalty, change management and performance improvement. The company's continual research points to best practices for workplace improvement, while its world-class trainers and coaches drive organizational and behavioral change at all levels and help people make the shift from learning to doing.

Leadership experts from The Ken Blanchard Companies are available for workshops and consulting as well as keynote addresses on organizational development, workplace performance, and business trends.

Global Headquarters

The Ken Blanchard Companies
125 State Place
Escondido, CA 92029
www.kenblanchard.com
1.800.728.6000 from the U.S.
+1.760.489.5005 from anywhere

Berrett–Koehler
Publishers

A community dedicated to creating
a world that works for all

Visit Our Website: www.bkconnection.com

Read book excerpts, see author videos and Internet movies, read our authors'
blogs, join discussion groups, download book apps, find out about the BK
Affiliate Network, browse subject-area libraries of books, get special discounts, and more!

Subscribe to Our Free E-Newsletter, the *BK Communiqué*

Be the first to hear about new publications, special discount offers, exclu-
sive articles, news about bestsellers, and more! Get on the list for our free
e-newsletter by going to **www.bkconnection.com.**

Get Quantity Discounts

Berrett-Koehler books are available at quantity discounts for orders of ten or
more copies. Please call us toll-free at (800) 929-2929 or email us at **bkp
.orders@aidcvt.com.**

Join the BK Community

BKcommunity.com is a virtual meeting place where people from around the
world can engage with kindred spirits to create a world that works for all.
BKcommunity.com members may create their own profiles, blog, start and
participate in forums and discussion groups, post photos and videos, answer
surveys, announce and register for upcoming events, and chat with others
online in real time. Please join the conversation!

Berrett–Koehler
Publishers

Berrett-Koehler is an independent publisher dedicated to an ambitious mission: *Creating a World That Works for All*.

We believe that to truly create a better world, action is needed at all levels—individual, organizational, and societal. At the individual level, our publications help people align their lives with their values and with their aspirations for a better world. At the organizational level, our publications promote progressive leadership and management practices, socially responsible approaches to business, and humane and effective organizations. At the societal level, our publications advance social and economic justice, shared prosperity, sustainability, and new solutions to national and global issues.

A major theme of our publications is "Opening Up New Space." Berrett-Koehler titles challenge conventional thinking, introduce new ideas, and foster positive change. Their common quest is changing the underlying beliefs, mindsets, institutions, and structures that keep generating the same cycles of problems, no matter who our leaders are or what improvement programs we adopt.

We strive to practice what we preach—to operate our publishing company in line with the ideas in our books. At the core of our approach is stewardship, which we define as a deep sense of responsibility to administer the company for the benefit of all of our "stakeholder" groups: authors, customers, employees, investors, service providers, and the communities and environment around us.

We are grateful to the thousands of readers, authors, and other friends of the company who consider themselves to be part of the "BK Community." We hope that you, too, will join us in our mission.

A BK Business Book

This book is part of our BK Business series. BK Business titles pioneer new and progressive leadership and management practices in all types of public, private, and nonprofit organizations. They promote socially responsible approaches to business, innovative organizational change methods, and more humane and effective organizations.